Some churches do 'ave 'em!

Some churches do 'ave 'em!

An A-Z of church life

David Gatward

Illustrated by Darren

Kevin Mayhew

First published in 1997 by
KEVIN MAYHEW LTD
Rattlesden
Bury St Edmunds
Suffolk IP30 0SZ

ISBN 0 86209 946 3
Catalogue No 1500089

0 1 2 3 4 5 6 7 8 9

Cover illustration and cartoons by Darren

Typesetting by Louise Hill
Printed and bound in Great Britain by
Caligraving Limited Thetford Norfolk

Dedication

This book is dedicated to all those who aren't afraid to laugh in church when the organist's wig starts to jiggle during the chorus.

Acknowledgements

In writing a book such as this a little artistic licence has to be taken. However, the inspiration stems from all my experiences as a 'son of the manse'. People such as the wondrous Mrs. Miggins or the slightly insane organist are exaggerations of the many people I have come to know and love as members of this wonderful family of the church. To list all those who have affected my growing would be impossible. All I can do is use this space to say a huge thank you to all those I have known throughout my church life for their influence and the experiences we have shared. From Sunday school teachers to youth group leaders. The old and wise, the young and mad. Coffee mornings, sponsored walks, youth services, drama, trips away and cold carol services. It is all part of what I am today; thank you.

I should also say a little thank you to my family. Living a life based on the church does funny things to some people and if you ever meet us, you'll understand what I mean. We may be slightly round the bend but I wouldn't swap it for anything.

Finally, cheers to Darren for his superb cartoons . . . 'Obi 1 has taught you well.'

Foreword

To me, God is someone with a huge smile who loves to laugh, play practical jokes and even chuckle at himself. The kind of God who knows that rain is not just necessary for an ecosystem but that it can be great fun to run through, and splash in its puddles. The kind of God who gives us the ability to be tickled (what use is there for this feature of our bodies other than to make us laugh?) The kind of God who makes faces in mirrors and understands how much fun it can be to throw food across a table as well as eat it. The kind of God who knows that if we are to be free creatures with a free will, we will by necessity have the freedom to hurt and to cry; so he redresses the balance a little.

Some find this a difficult concept. The idea that God can laugh at himself? Surely this is disrespectful? Not so, I think. We limit God to our self-made human conceptions of how we think our omniscient creator should behave. Why? Where else did we get this 'sense of humour' from? As the great David Kossoff mentions in one of his prayers, 'Humour didn't *evolve*, my scientists; the sense was *given*'. Now think about that! God gives us this sense of humour, to laugh at ourselves, each other, our mistakes, our troubles. What a great, great gift!

And so to this book. My life as a son of the manse has, I think, given me (and my two brothers!) a different look at the world of the church. Many see it from their pews and their groups; we saw it from the inside out. When your whole childhood has been in and around the church and its people you begin to look at things a little differently. The glasses are not rose-tinted or even stained glass, but perhaps a little distorted. Certain characters begin to pop up wherever you go. Certain activities, attitudes, ideas and hymn number rotas. In every church there are the young and the old, the confused and the certain, the dancers and the sitters. From crèche to quiche, Sunday school to the certainty of rain at any outside service, undecorated manse bathrooms to slide shows, chorus singing to dodgy drama. The church is full of the funny and the hilarious, even though at times it may not realise it. At times it takes itself far too seriously, unable to see the funny side of the youth group giggling as the preacher takes a sip from his 'pulpit glass' only to discover that someone got there first. At other times it ignores the fact that the choir's dramatic presentation of the shepherds visiting Jesus is positively hysterical. All the church needs to do is look in the mirror and pull a funny face, or perhaps throw a custard pie at itself and then jump around in a few puddles. The ability to laugh at ourselves and each other is as important as anything else we do as a family. Let's all start doing it a little bit more.

Abba

Our nearest equivalent is 'Daddy'. Nice thought really, calling God 'Daddy'. A lot more personal and affectionate. Not disrespectful either. It was his Son's idea after all (Mark 14:36). Now usually sung with great feeling (and possibly less understanding) in the familiar chorus, 'Abba, Father'.

Absent

As in '. . . from'. Often applied to the following:

1 Church
2 Coffee mornings
3 Choir practice
4 Mrs. Miggins' slide show on her years spent in outer Mongolia as a missionary to a tribe of pygmies.

Acne

Proof that God has a sense of humour although some of us find it hard to see the joke. Amazing ability to appear at just the wrong time. Prime examples include the night of your first date, and first job interview.

Acts

Book written about people who thought that God was pretty cool, especially as they'd got to know him through his Son. Jesus had done a lot for them and they did quite a lot for him. Notable 'acts' include being drunk in the street at 9am (Acts 2:13) – on the Holy Spirit, of course!

Adam

Father of the human race. Did not set a good example to his offspring. Remembered for running around naked in a garden with his wife, hiding from God, and having two sons, one of whom killed the other. (In fact, he had three sons but no one ever remembers Seth.) Adam basically hashed it up from the beginning, proving for ever that humans show little resilience when faced with temptation. It's no wonder dads have resorted to sitting in front of the fire wearing slippers, stroking the dog, smoking a pipe and watching TV. It's much safer.

Advent

The few weeks before Christmas marked by:

1 Far too many toy adverts on TV
2 Silly men dressed up as Father Christmas standing at every street corner
3 No snow at all
4 Huge overdrafts
5 Post-Christingle children with no hair (for *Christingle*, see below)
6 Cardboard calendars on kitchen doors designed specifically to cause arguments between children because 'Emma did it yesterday', 'It's my turn' and 'Owwwwwww, muuuuuummmm, pleeeeaaase!'

(N.B. People seem to have forgotten the real reason for Advent. Spiritual preparation is submerged and lost beneath a weight of tinsel and wrapping paper.)

Afterlife

Christianity's confidence in eternal life and happiness in heaven definitely has the edge over other possibilities, especially when compared with the idea of coming back to earth as a slug or something equally attractive.

Agony

Pain, though not necessarily physical. Listening to the fifth testimony in a row and singing 'Shine, Jesus, shine' *again* can be agony.

Ah-ha!

An exclamation sometimes used by preachers when they realise that their sermon actually has a point after all!

Alive

Many uses, for example:

1 'We are . . .'
2 'Jesus is . . .'
3 'I wish the choir were . . .'

Alleluia

Means 'Praise God'. Often used with 'Amen'. Frequently shouted by a certain sort of evangelist and over-zealous lay preacher. Sometimes used by the congregation at the end of the sermon (meaning 'Thank goodness that's over').

All Together Now

A popular phrase used by the following:

1 The choirmaster desperately trying to teach the church 'a really nice and modern up-beat chorus that the children will like'.
2 Sunday school teacher coaxing the children to *all* sing 'You in your small corner'.
3 Over-ambitious preacher who, wanting to make an impact by doing something really different, shouts, 'I want us *all together now* to give God a big round of applause (because I think it's a really cool and hip thing to do in church).'
4 Bored youth group who, being bored (again), decide that it would be much more amusing to make paper planes out of the notice sheet and throw them at the preacher. So: 'All together . . . NOW!'

Alone

How the preacher will have felt when, standing at the front of the church, he suddenly realised his flies were undone. The fact is that a person is never alone when they are with Jesus. This is due to his incredible ability to (and I quote) 'be with you always – even to the end of the age' (Matthew 28:20). He's often found residing within people. As long as the door is opened and he's invited in, he's not over-bothered about the current internal decor. He's more than happy to stay *for ever* and clean up the mess. Cool or what?

Altar

A table. That's it. That is what it is. A table. But it has reached that station in life that all tables aspire to. To be at the front of a church and have the honour of holding the cross and the sacrament. In fact, if you find that you are losing concentration during the service just focus on the cross and the sacrament and you'll find a whole lot to think and pray about.

Amazing

A number of uses. Most common include:

1 'Isn't God . . . ?'
2 'Isn't it . . . that the service finished early today?'

Rare uses include:

1 'That sermon was . . . !'
2 'Isn't quiche . . . ?' (usually after a faith tea)
3 'Aren't coffee mornings an . . . idea: full of vibrancy, originality and astounding value.'

Amen

Basically means 'I agree' and appears at the end of most prayers. Also used when a preacher says, 'I must draw to a close', resulting in a loud congregational outburst of 'Amen!'

Angry

Christians shouldn't be angry with other people. Difficult in the following situations:

1 Someone hits you
2 Someone teases you
3 Someone ignores you continually
4 Someone sits in the pew you've been sitting in for thirty-four years and your father before you . . .

Answer

Common in the phrase 'answer to prayer'. Also popular in 'answering God's call'. It must be noted that answers to prayer are nothing like phone calls. You can't just pick up a receiver and find God's voice at the other end. There are over five billion people on planet earth and he's got to talk to all of them! More often than not, the individual does not realise God has answered the prayer until *afterwards*. Another point: if you don't think God has answered, you're wrong. He just said 'No'.

Apostle

Jesus had twelve of them. Not to be confused with:

1 A pistol: that's a gun and Jesus wasn't a gangster
2 A postman: Jesus didn't have a black-and-white cat called Jess and didn't drive a small red van
3 A pollutant: Jesus was much more interested in purifying than polluting

Ask

As in Jesus' all-time classic, 'Ask, seek, knock' (Matthew 7:7). This must not, however, be used in the wrong context. Whereas it is perfectly OK to ask God for forgiveness and eternal life, it is wrong to ask him for a new bike for Christmas.

Attention

Definitely lacking in many youth groups during most services unless someone announces the singing of 'Come on and celebrate', or the child that has been running around the church for the last half an hour trips over.

Ayyyyymmeeeyyyeennnn

American pronunciation of Amen or just another exclamation from mad preacher. (See *Mad Preacher*.)

Bad

Three uses:

1 'That was . . .', as in 'that quiche really was very . . .'
2 'Not . . .', as in brother Richard's testimony 'wasn't . . .'
3 'I'm . . .', as in Michael Jackson

Balcony

If you are late you end up here. It is the worst seat in the house. Usually too warm because all the heat has risen from below. Often too far away from the minister to hear him, and the speaker behind you was never wired because 'we only use the balcony for latecomers or special occasions, so why bother?'

Bang

A noise that disturbs a service like nothing else can. Often caused by a book hitting the floor (see *Wally*), a child falling over (see *Attention*), or a member of the youth group hitting their head on the pew in front while manoeuvring into a comfortable praying position.

Barabbas

Will go down in history as 'most surprised man'. Having been caught red-handed as a terrorist and put on trial next to the Son of God, one would assume that the odds were not in his favour. Probably used the phrase 'Alleluia!' quite a lot after the incident.

Battleships

See *Games*.

Beg

Preferred description is 'collection' or 'offertory', but we know different.

Bible

Many aliases, such as:

1 The Word
2 The Way
3 The Truth
4 The Guide Book
5 God's Diary
6 The big boring book 'that I do read . . . honest' (and the opposite of boring if you actually do!)

Birth

God's way of saying the world will go on. Most women wish, however, that he'd chosen a less painful way of achieving it.

Black

Colour worn by many preachers, giving them the distinct likeness to a stick of liquorice.

Bored

As in 'I am . . .'. Favourite comment from the young people unless the service happens to be led by a young preacher called something cool like 'Nic the Vic' who plays lead guitar in a rock band and insists that Sunday morning is an excuse to sing 'Shine, Jesus, shine', clap hands, say 'Alleluia' a lot, and watch some very bad examples of acting.

Born Again

A common 'type' of Christian. Easily recognised by the following features:

1 Sandals
2 Flares
3 'Jesus loves me' smile
4 'Jesus loves me' badge
5 Huge colourful Bible

Favourite phrase is 'Have you found Jesus yet?' to which one must *not* reply,

'Why? Have you lost him?' (To find out what 'born again' really means see John 3.)

Brain

Wrong spelling of Brian. Also the most unused part of the anatomy (especially by members of the youth group during the sermon).

Brat

The child that runs around the church, burps (from both ends), has the noisiest toys possible, and belongs to absolutely nobody. (Part of the package deal with the church wally perhaps? – see *Wally*.)

Brave

What you are if you're daft enough to volunteer to look after the crèche.

Bread

Easily confused with cardboard when used at communion. This possibly proves the axiom 'man shall not live by bread alone'. Comes from 'Give us this day our daily bread' (implying that we wish to have real bread for communion and not that cardboard stuff, although 'give us our daily cardboard' isn't perhaps as meaningful).

Brian

Wrong spelling of brain. Also from *The Life of . . .*, a film by the Monty Python crew which we all know we shouldn't find funny but do because it is. Also a very sad name in the same league as George, Derek, Henry and David.

Brothers (and Sisters)

Colloquial term for everybody used by a guest speaker 'who's *really* evangelical'.

Bum

Numb as a result of sitting on the pews too long. There's no possible way you can sit comfortably on a pew. This isn't just a personal observation but a widely known fact. So what I and countless others would like to know is: Why on earth don't we have cushioned seats instead?

Burp

Really funny joke among the youth group during prayer time which induces a fit of giggling and, when stifled, results in a burp lasting for the rest of the service, causes more giggling, etc.

Called

Jesus called you to follow him and be his friend for eternity. Hard to believe but true. He called *you* – with all your grot, confusion, worry and problems. See? God does have a sense of humour!

Candles

An important aid to worship for some Christians. Candles look nice but they're really no more than an elaborately decorated lump of lard with a wick down the middle. Many shapes and sizes with different meanings:

1 I may be small, but put me in the hands of a child at Christingle and – POW! – Little Miss No Hair!
2 Average, cheap and available for those cold dark nights when all the lights go out
3 Arty, expensive and totally useless
4 Huge, top-heavy (and likely to topple), very expensive. Found in cathedrals or used as heaters in vicarages and manses

Canterbury
Where the Archbishop hangs out. Important bloke if you are Church of England and even if you aren't. The current one is renowned for singing 'Kum ba yah' and playing the tambourine. And rightly so too!

Carpenter
Jesus was one. (Not to be confused with a brother and sister singing duo.)

Catholic
Not Protestant. (Does God notice?)

Celebrate

From the all-time favourite song 'Come on and . . .'. This could be seen as rather a contradiction in terms when you consider the congregation singing it. You can see the questioning look upon their faces which says, 'What have I got to celebrate? I got up early on a Sunday to come and sit in a cold church on a hard pew and listen to old Mr. Jones trying to preach on the "Love Song of Solomon".' Of course, the real reasons, such as praising God, meeting other Christians and worshipping together, appear to fade away when faced with these 'really important, emotional, serious issues'. God must really want to tear his hair out on many a Sunday morning.

Chairs

Chairs are a good idea. Pews are not. Therefore it would be quite a logical step to replace the pews with chairs. For one reason or another this radical idea causes much dismay. This is understandable if the pews are attractive. Unfortunately, we have come across the flaw in the plan: they aren't. They look old, brown, uncomfortable and are all three. Yet even though the evidence has proven pews to be guilty on all charges, the jury is yet to be swayed.

Cheerful

What we aren't when getting ready for church knowing we're going to be late again. What we *are* once we get to church because everyone else is.

Chewing Gum

No matter where you are in church, under your seat will be a hard piece of mint-smelling, grey, 300-year-old chewing gum. No one really knows how it got there – especially as you are actually sitting in Mrs. Addlebury's seat and she's been there since the church was built. It's as if it breeds under pews. No matter where you are or where you go, it's there, gradually gaining consciousness, until one day you'll discover that the piece under your seat has gone and there in front of you stands a new preacher who, for some reason, has become stuck to the microphone and lectern . . .

Choruses

Modern hymns that may sound good. Given half a chance youth groups would sing them all the time and usually too fast. Choirs try to like them, attempt one or two to be 'hip', and sing them too slowly. Congregations are really a bit confused on the whole matter – especially when one week 'Shine, Jesus, shine' is sung at warp-speed by the youth group (accompanied by three guitars, drums, and clapping) and the next week it is sung sedately by the choir at an 'excuse me, but it really should be sung more slowly' speed (to the sole accompaniment of a pipe organ). It is worth remembering the 'Chorus Singing Code of Conduct' if you happen to stumble upon such a situation:

1 Smile
2 Stare at the ceiling or close your eyes

3 Clap hands a lot
4 Look at everyone else
5 Wear a twelve-string guitar
6 Say 'yes' and 'amen' during the instrumental bits

Christ

Was (and is) Jesus, Saviour, Lord of lords, King of kings, Prophet, Guide, Friend, Son of God, Conqueror of death and sin, miracle worker, cool dude with long hair. Need I say more?

Christening

Excuse for Mafia-type event when the whole family turns out not so much for the ritual dunking of Julia Anne, but for the huge booze-up that ensues. Also results in the whole congregation sitting outside as the family fill the church with their video cameras and children. (Seriously, it's God's way of saying how much the child is loved – not least by him.)

Christian

Someone who believes in Jesus as their saviour and is a vibrant, full-of-life, happy, confident, good-looking person. (Honest.)

Christingle

Cheap way to heat the church. Also a parent's nightmare. But it explains the Christmas event in a memorable way and it does look pretty!

Christmas

A multitude of events celebrating the birth of Jesus. Most people, however, seem to be much more interested in

1 'Wot's for dinner, Mum?'
2 'Look wot I got!'
and, on Boxing Day,
3 'I feel awful . . .'

Church

Usually describes a building in which you can praise God and sing 'Shine, Jesus, shine' over and over again. Also known in some areas as:

1 T' chapel
2 Bethel, Ebenezer or some other obscure Old Testament title
3 St . . . (add whatever name seems appropriate)
4 Church of the Everlasting Omnipotent Jesus Christ, Lord of lords, Forgiver of sins, and Sustaining River of Life, Peace, Love and Happiness

There are various types:

Type One is a small Victorian chapel with either three locals from the village, a dog and a ferret, or five hundred young people from a 'breakaway' church. In both cases the church is small, musty, too hot in winter and too cold in summer.

Type Two is a large church with impressive steeple or tower. Very cold. No congregation except for the choir, the vicar and the church cat (who plays the organ if Mr. Barnard can't make it).

Type Three is a modern church of hideous 1960s breeze-block design, cinema seats, a huge congregation and an impressive budget.

Type Four is a cathedral. Humungous, expensive to heat, old and beautiful. The bishop has his base there.

Coffee Morning

Popular fund-raiser which often seems to raise no money at all. Comes in the following guises:

1 Coffee Morning and Jumble Sale
2 Coffee Morning and White Elephant Stall
3 Coffee Morning and Bric-a-Brac
4 Coffee Morning and Bring-and-Buy Sale
5 Coffee Morning and Mrs. Miggins' slide show of her years spent in outer Mongolia as a missionary to a tribe of Pygmies

Cunning, isn't it? You can almost feel the excitement at the annual general, once a quarter, fund-raising committee . . .

'Anybody have any ideas for fund raising then?' asked the new vicar, trying to sound excited as well as enthusiastic. It was his first meeting with the infamous Mrs. Smith, Mrs. Bloombarn, Mr. Jenkins and Mrs. Miggins. This was 'The' fund-raising committee, the ones at the top when it came to innovative ideas, organisation and enthusiasm. Well, that's what he would have liked.

Anyway, this was his lot so he had better do something with it; unfortunately, ignoring it was not allowed. The problem was that Silence had managed to squeeze itself into the room as well and sat in the seat right next to him, taking over the meeting with an excited burst of absolutely no response whatsoever.

A bottom shuffled. A hand scratched. A throat swallowed. Cutting the silence with a sharp exclamation, Mrs. Bloombarn shouted, 'What about a coffee morning?' The vicar's heart sank. He'd been warned about this at college. The dreaded coffee morning disease which infects every church. No one is safe. No matter where you are, you'll meet it one day. This was that day. His very first church, his first meeting, and his first encounter with the 'Formidable Four'. Still, he had to pursue the idea. 'Good idea!' was all he could come up with, followed by 'Anything else?' Once again, Silence took the stage and proceeded to steal the show.

Until . . . 'How about my slide show?' squeaked Mrs. Miggins from behind her handbag, fluffy mittens and the duffel coat. Mrs. Bloombarn and Mrs. Smith congratulated her on the idea, and Mr. Jenkins volunteered to go and put the kettle on. The vicar sighed, put his excitement in a box and replaced it with 'I must get off, visiting to do, and a sermon to write. Can I leave that with you? Oh, good. See you next week.' With that he picked up his briefcase and ran as fast as politely possible out of the room and into the cool evening air.

Come, Follow Me

One of Jesus' favourite requests and still in use today. Hoped-for response is 'OK!'

Cross

God's way of showing how much he loved the world by allowing humankind to take his only Son and execute him on one. The most well-known part of the Christian message and still the hardest to take in. Many people wear a cross around their necks but, sadly, few seem to know why. (It must be noted that after three days Jesus rose from death, proving that if you follow Jesus, Satan hasn't got a chance.)

Crosses

As in 'noughts and . . .' (see *Games*).

Crucifixion

How humans thought they could deal with God . . . and got it wrong.

Cry

No service is complete without crying. This often comes from the child running around the church who has just tripped over the heater grating. Usually followed by a chorus of giggling from the youth group.

Also found to occur at large Christian rallies where big men at the front cry: 'ALLELUIA!' 'PRAISE THE LORD!' 'AYYYYMEN!' 'YOU ARE A SINNERRRRR!'

Dance

As in 'Lord of the . . .'. This may be true but dance is still taboo in many services. If it had been 'Lord of the extremely quiet and dull sermon' or 'Lord of the continuous squeal from a hearing aid during prayer', then there would have been few objections. Unfortunately, dance, being fun, rather noisy and requiring a lot of space, is still a no-no.

Daniel

Biblical Doctor Doolittle. Demonstrated in the all-time classic, 'The Lions' Den'.

David

Shepherd boy who made good – he became king of Israel! Notable achievements include killing a huge monster of a guy called Goliath, writing songs on the biblical equivalent of the guitar, having quite a few wives, and winning many battles. Basically, if one fancied being a king, David's way could sound attractive. He was also a character who knew God pretty well and as a result had someone to help sort out the frequent troubles he got into.

Days

As in 'the Last . . .'. No one knows when they will come. Jesus emphatically stated that *no one knows*. This has done little to stop the occasional idiot from having a guess. Such characters come in various guises, for example:

1 Every false prophet claiming to be Jesus and not being.
2 That bloke who used to commentate on football and now likes bright coloured clothes.
3 Mrs. Miggins.

Deliver

From the Lord's Prayer: 'Deliver us from evil'. People often find 'evil' to be too harsh a word and suggestions have been made that an alternative should be found, for example:

1 Deliver us from things that make us slightly perturbed
2 Remove us from that which is not good
3 Extricate us from ungodliness
4 Take away Mrs. Miggins. This was the favourite but when put forward at the church meeting it was turned down on the basis that coffee mornings (see above) would never be the same again

(Actually, looking at the way things are, the original version in the Lord's Prayer says it all.)

Deny

The apostle Peter is probably the most well-known individual who did this. He made the startlingly egotistical mistake of challenging God's son. He was certain that he would never deny Jesus, even though Jesus said, 'Oh yes, you will – and do it three times before the cock crows.' One could say Peter's chances of getting it right were slim – and they were.

Deuteronomy

An Old Testament book in which Moses talks to his people before nipping off heavenward at the ripe old age of 120 from the top of a mountain. There's a bit more to it than that, so read the book.

Disaster

General term for

1 Christingle, because 'Mum, my hair's on fire!'
2 Sunday School Survive (I mean Service) because 'Jenny *needed* the toilet'
3 Youth Group Service because 'it was too loud and they didn't sing "Jerusalem"'. (That's the one that starts with 'And did those feet in ancient time . . .'.)
3 Mrs. Miggins doing the children's address because she can't
4 The sermon because 'it always is and I'm usually asleep during the good bits'.

Discussion

A favourite of Sunday school teachers, youth groups and anyone attending courses entitled:

1 'Finding Yourself'
2 'Who Are You?'
3 'Have You Discovered Your Full Potential?'

Favourite phrases at these meetings are

1 'Use me as a sounding board'
2 'Thank you, Jason, that's a valuable point'
3 'Let's think about that for a moment'
4 'Anyone like to come in on that?'
5 'Mmmmmmmmm . . .'
6 'Ahhhhhhhhh . . .'
7 'Yeeaassss . . .'

These must all be accompanied by appropriate nodding of head, hand movements, and crossing of legs.

Distance

That vast expanse of empty pews between the pulpit and the first worshippers.

During

As in '. . . the sermon'. What you do if the point of the sermon was lost hours ago but the minister is still trying to drag it back. Ideas range from:

1 Getting all the youth group to stare at the preacher and make him paranoid
2 See who can make the nicest model from the notice sheet.
3 Play 'child busting'. Like cloud busting, except that you stare at a child and try to make it explode
4 Shout 'Amen' and 'Hallelujah' for no reason whatsoever

See *Games* for further ideas.

Easter
The reason for being a Christian. If Jesus can rise from the grave, then I guess he's worth listening to, obeying, following, etc. (See also *Crucifixion*).

Eat
Even though services last only about an hour, some people seem to find it necessary to take with them a store of supplies. These consist of boiled sweets and bags of mint imperials. Instead of openly admitting their guilt, they would rather try and open the sweet quietly. Of course, this is impossible and results in a five-minute session of 'I'm not making any noise by opening my boiled sweet really slowly – honest'. Another cunning ploy is to cough when placing the sweet in the mouth. Unfortunately, the effectiveness of this is lost when the person drops the sweet, resulting in yet another trip down 'Opening My Boiled Sweet' Lane.

Edition
The Bible's had squillions of these. From your standard 'Good News' to the computer bible. Small, large, black, white, colourful, English, French, Mongolian. You name it, it's been done! (And thank God for them all!)

Eggs
Staple fare at church breakfasts with the consistency of an egg-shaped lump of rubber. Completely tasteless yet no one really wants to say that they didn't enjoy it and thus upset the 'ladies who took a great deal of time to prepare this meal for us and we'd like to say thank you, wouldn't we?' (Applause.) These eggs also appear to breed in an enormous metal pan carried by a smiling old gentleman muttering excitedly, 'Come on, just one more!' Other attractions at this feast are cornflakes in bowls smaller than your tea cup, toast, jam (as long as you like marmalade) and four thousand gallons of tea.

Elijah
Hairy prophet dude found in Old Testament.

Emmanuel
One of Jesus' nicknames – very appropriate as it means 'God with us' which he is in Jesus. If looked at in a different light (preferably through really distorted glasses) it could read 'A Manual'. This actually makes a lot of sense. God is more or less our manual of life. He enables us to keep ourselves in running order, to spot any running problems, and generally to keep us in shape for the miles that lie ahead. He is even able to perform miracle restorations on what appear to be completely unrestorable examples of humanity – like you and me! So there you go, you've got further to go than any Volvo estate and harder paths to negotiate than the Paris-Dakar Rally, but you've got the best mechanic armed with the operator's manual, so buckle up and get ready for the ride of a lifetime!

Epistles
N.B. Not *Apostle* (see above). A fancy way of describing some letters written by characters such as Paul.

Eve
Wife of Adam. Set just as bad an example as he did. Listened to a snake (obvious really – a snake knowing more than God), disobeyed God, ran around naked with her husband . . . you know the rest.

Evening
As in '. . . Service'. The one no one seems to go to except for the old lady at the back who has failed to wake up from morning worship, the organist and Mrs. Miggins. The preacher is actually an inflatable replica of 'Mr. Edwards,

a preacher from Wigan' backed by a recording of the morning service. There are the occasional successes, such as youth rallies, concerts, united do's and slide shows. (Oh, hello Mrs. Miggins!)

Ever

As in 'for ever and . . .'. Extremely long time. Far too long for our poor brains to cope. Still, God says he'll be with us for ever and we're not exactly in a position to argue.

Exodus

The story of Moses who rescued a whole nation from slavery, led them through the wilderness to settle in the promised land. A veritable biblical combination of Crocodile Dundee and Superman. Cool! (See also *Moses*.)

Exorcism

Dealing with Satan first-hand and giving him the proverbial kick up the backside. Only to be undertaken by those who really know what they're doing, and not by anyone who happens to be wearing a cross and has the ability to say, 'In the name of God be gone, foul shadow!' This would be like entering the boxing ring blindfolded, walking up to Evander Holyfield and calling him a 'lard ball who couldn't box his way out of a paper bag'. All in all an extremely unwise act.

Ezekiel

Another hairy prophet (see *Elijah*).

Faith

What we have in Jesus, except when he seems to go wrong and we know best. We really are stupid, aren't we?

Faith Tea

A gathering of people who get together before or after any service to share a meal. Everyone smiles and pretends to ignore the fact that they could actually be at home having a Sunday roast or whatever. Instead, they are faced with the classic feast of quiche, baby sausage rolls and very small cakes that 'were baked only yesterday. No really, they were.' There is always an ample supply of tea, and various people you've never seen before. Faith teas? We love em!

Family

As in '. . . of God'. We are all one family, brothers and sisters (of all shapes, colours, races and sizes) in Jesus with one Father: God. However, a visitor may be inclined to believe otherwise when looking at many churches. The choir want to sing and so do the youth group; so-and-so's sitting in Mr. Greavel's pew and he's none too pleased; the sermon was too long – but any less and it would have been too short; and then there's still Mrs. Miggins and her slide show. Still, every family has its disagreements!

Famous

A type of Christian like no other. They are often wealthy, have Colgate-clean teeth, no blemishes and they love Jesus a lot. A typical example is Cliff Richard who is incredibly nice all the time, gives vast amounts of money to charity, and smiles a lot. His other notable achievements include 'We're all going on a summer holiday', 'Mistletoe and wine', and having a top lip that quivers.

Far Away

Many people think God is – we know he isn't. This is backed up by Jesus saying he'll stay closer than a brother and live in our hearts for eternity. Unfortunately, humanity has failed once again to grasp the simplest of ideas. This is displayed in such staggering examples of stupidity as 'The Tower of Babel'.

Feast

Absolutely any meal that isn't a faith tea – in other words, no quiche, baby sausage rolls, dry fish paste sandwiches or small hard chocolate cakes.

Feeding

As in '. . . of the five thousand'. One of Jesus' all-time blockbusters. Feeding five thousand people with the equivalent of a mid-afternoon snack is quite something, never mind the leftovers. Of course, people have said that this wasn't actually a miracle at all, and that there was in fact enough food to go round. The flaw in this is that if the people had food why did it take a little boy and his lunch to spark off the fact that eating theirs would be a good idea too. Also, if they had food why did no one else own up when Jesus asked the obvious trick question: 'Anyone got anything to eat?'

Feet

As in 'Jesus washed his disciples' . . .'. This proves a few things. He's humble, ready to do anything to show the extent of his love, unafraid of getting dirty, good for a laugh and, if my feet are anything to go by, completely devoid of a sense of smell.

Fellowship

Favoured word, often used to describe a service which contains choruses, testimonies, lots and lots of 'amens' and 'alleluias' and a 'message' (fancy name for a sermon).

Find

As in 'seek and ye shall . . .'. This is all very well but the confusion lies in the actual seeking. What are you trying to find? Yourself? Is that such a good idea? Is it really worth it? Many believe it is, of course, and spend lots of time exploring their 'inner self'. They search in desperation for that hidden answer to lead them to understand who they really are. Shame that they ignore the obvious way to go about it – just ask Jesus. Seek and ye shall find the big guy who knows and understands you better than you can ever hope to. Go on, try it.

First

As in 'the last shall be . . .'. Often used out of context by really 'funny' people at the back of the queue for the faith tea who push to the front. All I can say is they're welcome to my place.

Font

Sort of a fondue for babies with a lot more significance than getting your fingers burnt and covered in cheese while trying to hold a pretentious dinner party with people you don't really like that much.

Forecast

The annual church garden fête depends on this. The well-rehearsed comment from the week before is always along the lines of 'Well, I hope the weather forecast is good this year. Better start praying!' No one seems to realise that it *always* rains. Even changing the date of the fête to another day does no good. It is always sunny at the beginning until the official opening, then – BOOM! – there's one almighty clap of thunder which introduces the heaviest downpour in living memory. The really amazing thing is that people still turn up! No one knows who they are or where they're from, they just arrive out of nowhere, mutter, 'Oh, isn't it a shame about the rain?', buy everything at hand and then disappear. It's as if they aren't actually real people. Maybe it's one of those emergency kits for rainy days. Scatter a few of the special seeds at the side of each stall and if it rains . . . INSTANT CROWD!

Forgiveness

God's really got this sussed. He loves us so much that, no matter what we've done, he's willing to forgive us. (He must be quite something. I know I wouldn't forgive me.) Anyway, even though this is the case, people are still unconvinced. Why? Everyone's done something bad. Surely everlasting forgiveness should bring the crowds in? Sad thing is, most don't realise they need it.

Fridge

Every church kitchen has one. Usually donated by someone (no one knows who) who thought it would be useful. Why? It's never used and hasn't even had a plug on it for the last five years. Mind you, it really comes into its own

on those coffee mornings when Mrs. Miggins uses it to store the groceries she's just bought from the supermarket so that she can get on with serving the coffee. Ingenious, until she forgets about her food supply. Three weeks later half a pound of mouldy bacon and a pound of even mouldier Stilton reveal the source of the unpleasant smell permeating throughout the church.

Funny

The most popular preachers aren't always those who are ultra-spiritual but usually those who are funny. Unfortunately, their humour isn't always intentional. They stand at the front of the church and smile inanely at the congregation. The point of the sermon is often lost because those who are listening are much more interested in the rather disconcerting way the preacher keeps picking up his Bible only to move it a quarter of an inch to the left or right. He then wiggles his ear, shuffles his feet and sniffs.

You may also notice how really funny a congregation can be. The sermon is dragging on, your bum has lost all feeling and suddenly out of the corner of your eye you see . . .

1 Mr. Jones snoring
2 Mrs. Addlebury hiding her book on gardening in her Bible and reading it very happily
3 The child running around the church examining what appears to be a dead cat, but is actually the wig off the now bald Mr. Jones
4 The organist who, thinking no one can see him where he's sitting, picks his nose. He forgot about that small mirror next to him which he uses to keep an eye on the preacher.

Games

Played during dull sermons, slide shows, christenings, and at any other time you're bored. They're graded, not on the basis of playability but on their disturbance factor. Many of the activities aren't really games but 'ways of passing the time'. Wherever you stand on this, here are a few helpful examples you can use:

1 Eavesdropping: especially entertaining when sitting behind 'the two who talk all the time during absolutely everything'. Vital information (such as the fact that Sarah Williams has acquired extra spuds at the local vegetable stall for three weeks running, and Jonathan Brown 'really has grown, hasn't he?') can be gleaned from these two pools of pointless information.

2 Holding your breath: timeless and as popular now as it was many years ago. The participants are easily spotted. They're the ones who glow purple, looking as though they've sat on Mrs. Miggins' hat pin, and suddenly expel four gallons of air. Unfortunately, when too many people take part it can turn the church into something resembling a train station full of loudly deflating bouncy castles.

3 Paper aeroplanes: why do churches give out notice sheets? They don't last five minutes. Where it tells you that Mr. Jenkins is back with another 'fun-filled, exciting look at the gospels' coincides exactly with the folding line for the making of the perfect projectile.

4 Sucking sweets (see also *Eating*): one variation is to try and make the sweet last for the whole sermon. Always beware if the preacher has managed to sing the first three hymns in the first ten minutes – you're in for a long battle.

5 Shoe laces: assume praying position and tie your neighbour's shoes together. If accomplished it can prove to be devastating during communion or if they've got to read the next lesson.

6 Count bits of stained glass: well, you really have reached the bottom of the pile, haven't you? Still, a sermon comparing modern-day philosophical views with those of the early existentialists is hardly to be classed as an attention grabber.

7 Preacher paranoia: a classic! Simple and effective. The more people involved, the greater the effect. All you have to do is stare at the preacher. Not a normal stare but one of those 'I'm going to make you explode' stares. If the whole youth group joins in the effect is tenfold. (Count things such as the number of times he wipes his brow and moves his Bible.)

8 Child Busting: see *During*.

9 Battleships: another use for the notice sheet. Variations include drawing a map of the church with chosen victims drawn in and you have the power to zap them when you so desire. You can also think of possible 'last words' said by the victims such as 'What about the quiche?' and 'But I've got to take the collection'.

10 See who can get every single joint in their body to make a cracking sound. Note how the knuckle joint of the middle finger echoes during prayer time.

11 Inflicting pain: on the words 'Let us pray' squeeze your neighbour's leg as hard as possible. Wonderful muffled screams will ensue, followed by a number of death threats because 'I can't believe you did that!'

12 Shadows: see if you can put that shadow which looks like a dead pigeon right on the preacher's nose.

13 Watch blindness: sun + watchface = dazzled preacher.

14 Dares: beware as the disturbance level breaks all rules! Dare someone to swap the hymn numbers, challenge your neighbour to drink the water from the pulpit, replace the Bible on the lectern with a copy of *Delia Smith's Complete Cookery Course*.

15 Write a book and become an incredibly wealthy and well-known author – like I'm not!

Garden of Gethsemane

Where Jesus had his final talk with his Father before facing the cross. It was while he was in the Garden that he was arrested by a squad of heavies accompanied by the winner of 'the most unpopular person of the millennium' competition, Judas. Not satisfied with selling Jesus for a pittance, Judas went on to identify him to his enemies with a kiss – the sign of friendship. Peter, being the kind of person he was, wasn't impressed, and responded in the only way he thought appropriate by throwing his weight around. The effect was hardly heroic as he only managed to cut off some poor squaddie's ear! There's nothing like cool-headedness to solve a crisis – and Peter's reaction was nothing like it! The only one to remain calm was Jesus. Once more he stands head and shoulders above everyone else. Just read John's account of the incident, and you'll see what I mean in the words of Jesus' prayer.

Gatward

How did that get in here?

Gave

As in 'God . . . his only Son to be our Saviour'. Isn't God's love quite something?

Genesis

The first book in the Bible (not to be confused with a certain well-known rock band). Contains great stories such as the one about Noah as well as the well-known bodge by Adam and Eve. Now Noah really was an extraordinary fellow. Not many people live to 950 and build a wooden version of the *QE2* in their back gardens. No doubt he got rather annoyed with jokes such as:

1 'Do you think it's going to rain then, Noah?'
2 'Planning to build a pond then?'
3 'Isn't it a bit big for the pond in the park?'

He must have had a very good sense of humour. Just imagine if 'Hey Noah, I want you to build an ark' had actually been a misinterpretation of 'Hey Noah, I want you to build a house'. No doubt Noah thought that a house wasn't up to God's usual standards of grandeur and decided a huge three-storey boat would be much more appropriate. If this is the case, then I guess God would have been pretty surprised at the question, 'OK, I've built the boat in the middle of the desert. Now what?' A flood was really the only way to avoid Noah winning the prize as the 'Builder of the most pointless object ever constructed'.

Ghost

As in 'Holy . . .'. This really does confuse things. People can just about cope with the Father and Son part of the equation, but this ghost business really is beyond them. You can be filled with it, blessed by it, and baptised in it – but you can't see it. Great! Well, God tells us it's a he and not an it, and that he's there, so I'm not arguing.

Gift

As in 'a . . . from God'. According to the Bible we've all been given a gift from God. These range from healing to speaking in tongues. The trouble is that we can forget that everyone else has a gift as well, be it as simple as the ability to listen or make people happy. It's not just the 'biggies' that are important. In fact, some are over-rated. Speaking in tongues can be classed as a 'biggie'. This is a gift that enables you to worship God in an unknown language that originates in heaven. It can, however, be rather confusing for the newcomer to some churches when they suddenly find the person next to them mumbling away and emitting strange sounds while everyone else murmurs 'Yes', 'Amen' and 'Alleluia'! The trouble is that it can sound as if they've just ordered the weirdest pizza possible and are now asking for 'extrarel ishand cu cum ba'. Why don't they just use the tried and tested 'Amen' or 'Praise the Lord'? Still, God knows what they mean and how they feel.

Give

As in 'Would you like to . . . a hand with the Sunday School Service?' or 'Would you like to . . . your testimony?' This involves you passing on something that you have. In the case of Sunday Schools it would probably be very close to giving away your life – especially if you've got the Jameson twins. As far as testimonies go, well it's up to the individual. If you want to destroy your credibility as a human being then you stand up and gibber for five minutes. Alternatively, you could actually wake up that woman at the back next to the heater by really saying what Jesus has done in your life!

God

Now come on!

Goodness

We as Christians are full of this. (Well, we should be.) Unfortunately, most of us are running on empty tanks and God isn't a gas station where we can just go along and top ourselves up. Goodness is what you could call a self-sufficient commodity. It's up to us to keep it topped up and, with the help of the Holy Spirit and prayer, to fix those ever-persistent running repairs. We should never hit empty!

Gormless

The expression on the congregation's faces *all the time!*

Great

God is and we are not.

Habakkuk

One of the Old Testament's lesser-known prophets, with a name that rarely appears in the top-ten list of the most likely names to feature in a Christening (see above) service.

Haggai

Ditto.

Hall

Where would we be without the church hall? The place that offers a pool of resources which defies the dreams and imagination of any minister or vicar. Well, it would do if it hadn't been built four hundred years ago, didn't leak, had heating that worked, a piano that was in tune, a sensibly sized kitchen, and was actually the right size to play badminton in. For some reason the church is always built perfectly but somehow the builders always get the hall wrong, almost as if it's an afterthought . . .

Bill stood back and admired his work. 'Three years,' he thought. 'Three years of back-breaking work. Finished at last.' The church stood out against the fading summer sky, a silhouette of craftsmanship standing out against the masterpiece of the Creator, filling Bill's heart with pride. Soaking up the beauty of his creation one last time, he turned and slowly made his way back home. A small figure against the night sky. Then suddenly it dawned on him – '. . .*!! I forgot to build the hall!!' (* What was to appear here was censored by the publisher who is always aware of the reader's sensitivities.)

Halo

(N.B. Not *Hello* – see below.) Remember when *The Saint* was on the box? (If you do you can't be a teenager and should be congratulated on reading this book.) Well, Simon Templar always appeared with a halo. If you ask me, though, I reckon it would get in the way. What happens when you're having a shower and it gets wet? Will it short-circuit? Will it shrink? If a person really is a saint they don't need a halo as the love of Jesus in them will shine through anyway.

Happy

Becoming a Christian doesn't automatically guarantee that you'll feel this way (contrary to the old Sunday School chorus 'I'm H - A - P - P - Y', although singing the chorus did help your spelling in primary school). Jesus tells us that we must be prepared to take up our 'cross' if we're serious about following him and being a disciple. What that meant – as anyone who had watched the Roman occupying army going about its business would know – was that the prospective Christian had to be ready to face rejection, torture and even death for their beliefs. It's hardly any wonder that after three years' hard graft Jesus still only had a handful of loyal friends (and even some of them weren't up to much when the chips were down). Even now the 'career prospects' don't seem that appealing unless you're an out-and-out masochist.

Obviously it's not like that. All Jesus is saying is that if you really love someone you'll go to the end of the world for them: nothing will be too demanding; no cost will be too great. He proved the truth of this on the cross, especially in the way he reacted to it. He forgave everyone who'd been involved from those who'd hammered in the nails to those who cooked up the charges just to get rid of him. Even after he'd been treated so cruelly, he still came back and rose from the dead. That's some love he has for us! All he asks is that we'll love him as much in return. Is it so much to ask or expect? Who wants a cushy number anyway? Climbing mountains and shooting rapids are both dangerous and considered foolhardy by many, but the exhilaration, the sense of really living and achieving something is unsurpassed – that is, except by following Jesus. Life is meant to be an adventure not a spectator's seat securely protected on the sideline. It's in setting out on the 'Jesus adventure' that happiness is found. Hard core, or what?

Heaven

God's pad. From all accounts, a good place to go, although I wouldn't mind knowing a bit more about it, especially as Jesus says that all who trust him will be spending eternity there. I mean, what on earth (sorry, if we're dealing with eternity should that be 'off earth' or 'outside earth'?) are we going to do with ourselves? Mind you, if we try and answer that then we get into the 'in heaven there will be no time' talk and the 'if you can describe heaven or eternity then they've ceased to be either' sort of statement. This can all get rather confusing.

For example, time and the speed of light are interrelated. If you were to travel faster than the speed of light then you would, in theory, travel through time as you are going faster than time itself. On that assumption, we could assume that before creation there was no time because light as we know it did not exist. So perhaps we could say that before the creation of the universe there was nothing. Trouble is, what was this nothing? A very large space? The beginning of eternity? (Can eternity have a beginning?) Well anyway, in the beginning there was nothing and then it exploded, creating light and, as a result, time. Thus, if heaven is in another dimension then light may not exist as such and time would therefore be devoid of meaning. Eternity could, therefore, mean living in a place where time does not exist. In effect, if there is no time, eternity isn't really that long, but if it was, then it would be very long indeed. Confused yet? I think I'll stick to listening to Jesus, who makes much more sense, and I'll just have to wait a bit longer (and I don't mind if it's quite a bit longer) before I find out personally what heaven really is like.

Hell

Opposite of heaven (i.e. hell is Satan's pad). According to the Bible it's hardly likely to feature in any holiday or tourist guide (although from what I've heard of some holidays it sounds very similar). Contrary to what we may want to believe, Jesus seemed to say that as a place it does exist, and that it's to be avoided at all cost. The way to do that is to believe in him and live in the way that he taught.

Hello

(N.B. Not *Halo* – see above.) Whenever you go to a church where you're not known you're likely to be confronted by the 'welcomers'. They genuinely care about people and express it with warmth and affection. They want you to feel at home, to feel that you're among friends. They're lovely people, but they can sometimes get a bit too enthusiastic in their welcoming which then comes out like this: 'Hello!Howareyou?Ohgood,andwhereareyoufrom?Really?Well IhopeyouhaveanicetimewithusandthatGodwillreallyblessyouinourworshipth ismorning.' It's all said without taking a single breath as they pump your hand up and down and look over your shoulder to see if they've missed any other visitor that has tried to slip past them.

They never stop smiling and everything you say (when you can get a word in) is 'very, very interesting'. You could tell them that for breakfast you ate three plates of moussaka with a vanilla slice and cold gravy, and that you've only come to watch the gherkins do the waltz backwards wearing pyjamas! They'd still stand there smiling and say, 'HowinterestingandIhopeyouenjoyyourvisit.'

The church can be a funny place and many of us who attend it might be described in the same way – but aren't God's people great?

Help

A favourite word, frequently used by those organising something. Organising has nothing to do with work. To organise means to delegate – in other words, give other people the jobs so you don't have to do anything! Prime examples are to be found throughout the Church. It can often seem that everyone is in charge of something which means everyone is delegating, resulting in everyone doing nothing. (This is often the function of committees.) Of course the one who delegated everything in the first place was the vicar. Trouble is, because everyone else is delegating, they go to the vicar for help ('Well, he does have plenty of time, and I'm so busy') and the poor guy, already overworked, ends up doing even more! A crazy situation which, because it's self-perpetuating, seems impossible to resolve. The Bible says something about the Church being a body, with each part fulfilling its function and supporting all the other parts in what they do – such radical thinking might dispose of many committees, make the Church more effective, and actually allow the vicar to have a day off now and then.

Hiccups

The 'Curse of Hiccups' is well known in preaching circles. It can strike anybody at any time. There are a variety of ways to deal with the problem:

1 The 'No, I haven't got hiccups, honest, no really' approach. Hold your breath, trying to stop the hiccup as it comes up. It doesn't work. For some reason, however, people believe that it does. Why? The only effect it usually has is to make the sufferer burp. Great, a real blockbuster of a solution. Get

rid of the hiccups and replace them with something even more embarrassing and audible.

2 The 'I know how to stop hiccups' approach. Stand on your head, recite Shakespeare and drink four gallons of water. Makes you look stupid, however, doing this three rows from the front of the church in full view of both the preacher and the choir (who themselves are all trying to stop giggling and as a result are prime candidates for a bout of the hiccups).

3 The 'Look at me, everyone, I've got hiccups' approach. Stand up, open your mouth and hiccup as loud as humanly possible. For added effect, hold your breath thus causing excessive burping too. You'll end up looking decidedly ridiculous, get on everyone's nerves and sound something like three hundred frogs on heat hopping down the Mersey tunnel. This is guaranteed, however, to bring the sermon to a speedy end endearing you even more to everyone concerned, except the preacher.

Hope

The opposite of hopeless. To get the basic idea, read *Hopeless* and leave out the negative words, replacing them with a positive version. For example, 'without hope' becomes 'with tea'. Still confused? If so, read on.

Hopeless

'Without hope' or, in the case of the Methodist church, 'without tea'. It is a well-known fact that without tea a Methodist is indeed without hope. If you believe this to be an exaggeration, it proves (a) that you're not a Methodist and (b) that you need to go and observe this denominational feature for yourself. Every activity revolves around that essential cup of tea. Tea after the service, tea after the prayer meeting, tea during the slide show, tea with the collection, tea with tea. Of course it's not your average tea. This stuff is brewed in mutated kettles the size of cement mixers to a secret recipe known only to a select few. Members of this small elite force are the only people capable of brewing the beverage to the correct colour (something between the colour of tar and rusty ironwork) and consistency (something akin to tar that's likely to dissolve the rusting ironwork) and they all look the same. Sweet smiling face, biceps like Arnold Schwarzenegger, and the selling power of the whole stock market put together. Their motto? Yep, you've guessed it: 'Who pours wins'.

Hymns

First of all, why is it spelt like this? Was it an early version of the deliberate misspelling favoured by many bands who, trying to be cool, spell their band name wrong. Remember The Byrds who cunningly substituted the 'i' with a 'y' – maybe that's what the Church was into a few hundred years ago. Great, isn't it – and someone came up not only with 'hymns' but also 'psalms'. Somehow, though, I think there must be a more plausible suggestion floating around somewhere. Other than that, they are the songs that everyone likes to sing (especially from the comfort of their armchair where they sit warmed by their fire and Harry Secombe on the TV) – that is unless they belong to the youth group who think (only occasionally, of course), 'If it's not by Graham Kendrick [see *Kendrick* below] then it must be boring and old-fashioned.' There are a few that achieve that 'favoured by the young people' status and include 'Jesus is Lord' and that one with 'my chains fell off' in it. (Actually, if some adults were honest they'd probably agree with the youth group.)

I Am

Widely used phrase in all circles of the Church's life. Jesus said, 'I am the way, the truth and the life.' Most of us, however, sometimes feel like replying, 'I am the lost, the not so sure and the spiritually unconscious.'

Impossible

According to God, absolutely nothing is impossible. All we need is faith the size of a grain of mustard seed and we can move mountains. Being small-minded humans we define mountains as those humungous lumps of rock which people who enjoy freezing to death and living on nothing but porridge seem to love getting lost on! Of course, God was talking metaphorically (I hope!). He was pointing towards the mountains of our lives – all the troubles and pitfalls, the disappointments and confusions. If we have faith even the size of a mustard seed then we can and will see it through and meet with God on the other side of the Everest of our lives. See, you aren't doing so badly after all! (See you at the summit!)

In Conclusion

The most eagerly awaited phrase at any meeting. This is rather strange as it is so rarely used. It is a well-known fact that preachers rarely conclude and even if they do then you miss it because you are either asleep, playing games (see *Games*) or trying to count the number of hairs on Mr. Grange's head! The fact is that very few preachers understand the meaning behind 'conclude' in the sense of 'to bring to a point and finish'. It's as if a sermon isn't so much a thing that you create and form and hold together but something that comes to life on a piece of paper with its only aim being to lead the preacher around in circles and confuse the congregation! The most amazing fact of all is that if you go along with an open mind and actually expect to get something out of it, then you will more than likely come away with a feeling that God was there too and actually said something to you! Don't you just love him?! (All together now: 'Yes!')

Insect

You know, the one that is approximately a hundred metres across, sounds like a Tornado taking off, and divebombs you and absolutely no one else for the duration of the service! If it gets bored with this, it then decides that escape would be a very good idea and proceeds to batter itself senseless against the stained glass windows. I think that it is about time God told the insect world that it is actually impossible to fly through glass!

Insignificant

We think we are and God knows we are not. That's the great thing about God. We look in the mirror and see a reflection of someone who's nearest equivalent is a compost heap – a pile of festering, rotting, unwanted rubbish. Disgusting, smelly, unsightly and usually hidden in a corner behind a cunningly deceptive attractive facade. But good old God looks at us in a way only he can. He sees straight through the false attractive front and right into the compost heap. But instead of seeing a pile of useless smelly rubbish he sees a mass of colourful flowers! Just like any good gardener he knows just how useful compost really is. Although we may be just a pile of garbage, in God's eyes we are all potential Gardens of Eden. All we need is a few seeds (Hope-eticus, Faith-iarus, Glory-itis, Love-onia, etc.) and a decent gardener (Hi, God!). Then perhaps out of the rubbish of ourselves a few flowers will begin to grow!

Intercession

One of those 'if all else fails' type of activities. If a service isn't going to last that crucial hour (and pity the preacher if that happens and Mrs. Miggins is there) it is advisable to pull out 'Prayers of Intercession'. This involves praying for anybody and anything interspersed with the aptly titled 'times of silence'. These pan out the time and allow the preacher time to try and find a concluding point for his sermon!

Isaiah

One of the many hairy prophets who spent their lives posting verbal signs for God and were generally ignored. Times haven't changed much, have they?

Janet

My mum who deserves a mention just for putting up with me all these years!

J.C.

Really cool, hip and trendy name for Jesus. Often used by the youth group and various radical T-shirt companies wanting to show that Jesus isn't boring at all and did in fact invent the idea of making your name sound really cool by shortening it to just the initials! So, M.C. Hammer, L.L. Cool J. and all you others, bow down to the Hippest Creator of all Eternity: J.C. King, Lord of Lords (and my best mate!).

Jesus

What can I say? He is the one who promised to be with us for all eternity and I don't know about you but I think that this warrants a huge round of applause! Why? Well, I don't see how anyone would want to spend eternity with the likes of me! I'm a grotty, smelly ratbag of a guy who tries to be a Christian and fails all the time. But Jesus accepted me as I was and as I am. I will never ever reach perfection. I will stumble and fall continuously along life's rocky road, making mistakes left, right and centre. The difference is that Jesus will always be there to pick me up, brush me down and set me on my way. When he said he would never leave us, he meant it. This is a contract that cannot be broken. He doesn't just pack his bags and leave as soon as we make our first mistake; he sticks by us and helps us tidy up the mess. Don't you just love him?

Job

The winner of 'The Most Unlucky Person Ever' competition! If something was going to go wrong then without doubt it would happen to poor old Job. If you ever think that things are going badly then just read this account of a man who followed God to the hilt, lost everything and still never gave in. See, it isn't that bad after all, is it?

John

Writer of one of the greatest lines in the Bible: 'For God so loved the world that he gave his only Son so that anyone who believes in him shall not perish but have eternal life' (John 3:16). Now is that something worth shouting about or what? (At this point the reader is requested to stand and shout out very loudly, 'I love you, Lord' or, if not truly acquainted with the Big Guy Upstairs, to stand up and scream with all your heart, 'I want to love you, Lord!' YIPPEE!)

Joke 1

At last, a word that isn't a person! There is very little that can do more to break the monotony of a really boring sermon than the whispering of a joke to one's peers. Even if the punchline is lost it usually results in a trip to giggle city as the joke is passed down the line! It is a weird fact of life that if the conditions are right then giggling becomes an unstoppable epidemic. These conditions appear to consist of hard uncomfortable pews, boring preachers, no heating and at least four or five teenagers. The result is a mass of backs that appear to have developed really bad hiccups as their shoulders bounce up and down uncontrollably in time to a sound that has a distinct likeness to thirty gagged hyenas who have just witnessed the funniest thing ever (see *Noah*). Well, you've got to laugh, haven't you?!

Joke 2

Cunning ploy used by inventive lay preachers and reverends to lull the congregation into a false sense of security in the belief that the sermon may be good after all. Jokes can be introduced with the following phrases:

1 'That reminds me . . .'
2 'A few weeks ago . . .'
3 'I've probably told you this one but . . .'
4 'Ermm, err, mmm, well, there was this . . .'

Preachers are very rarely put off by the fact that congregations do not laugh. No one knows why this is so, but it is a widely known fact that, wherever you are, even Mr. Strombard with his 'really funny hat, glove puppet and hilarious visual aid' couldn't raise a whimper. Suggested reasons for this phenomenon are:

1 'Church isn't a place for laughter'
2 'Christianity isn't supposed to be funny'
3 'God doesn't like jokes'

If these are true then it's difficult to understand the two old ladies at the back of the church who commence every service by shouting 'Has he started yet?' and then comment after the sermon (in a multi-decibel whisper) 'He's not very good, is he?' Who needs jokes?

Jonah

Now here was a guy who was really keen on doing his utmost to follow God's every instruction, and to demonstrate this he decided that a good plan of action would be to run away! Not really the cleverest of acts but, never mind, you've got to admire his courageous attitude even if he could beat off all opposition in the fight for the winner of 'The Stupidest Idea by Anyone Ever' competition! Unsurprisingly, God followed him on to a boat sailing for Tarshish and, in reply to Jonah's 'Yes, of course I'll do that, God, but I must just go on a round-the-world cruise first, if you don't mind!', set off a huge storm which scared the rest of the crew silly! Jonah was eventually found out as the culprit and promptly thrown overboard. It is here that God shows us his best example of sheer theatricalness by having Jonah swallowed by a very large fish which spat him out on a beach three days later! Jonah eventually got the message and carried out the job at Nineveh, making God very pleased indeed. And the message of this story? If God tells you to do something, then you'd better do it. (Well, I'm not keen on being swallowed by a fish!)

Joshua

Contains one of the classic stories from the Old Testament. This is where God shows Joshua a whole new approach in tactical invasion. Instead of plumping for the usual use of battering rams, siege towers and the like, God decides that a more theatrical approach was necessary. He tells Joshua to gather together his entire army and to walk around the city of Jericho for six days. This was presumably to psych out the enemy. Following this, on the seventh day they would walk around it seven times to the tune of the priests blowing the trumpets. Then, after a final long blast, the entire army would give an almighty shout and the walls would come tumbling down. God really does like to do things differently, doesn't he?

Joy

What the congregation is filled with when they actually recognise a song and tune which a visiting preacher has chosen for the service!

Kendrick, Graham

Hailed as the new King David. His new approach to singing songs to God has caused a sudden increase in the sales of twelve-string guitars and tambourines, as well as a need for new floors in many churches to cope with the renewed interest in dancing and jumping up and down a lot while praising God! Youth groups love him (after all, these are songs that you can use real instruments in, such as electric guitars and drum kits!) and the rest of the congregation appears to be enjoying it just as much. And God? Well, I reckon there's a great big grin right across that wonderful face as we all sing together to him – no matter what the song!

Kill

As in 'Thou shalt not . . .'. Other uses include:

1 Thou shalt not . . . the tune to this song by playing it in the wrong key, at the wrong speed and at the wrong moment (for example, the funeral march as the bride enters the church).
2 Thou shalt not . . . the congregation by drowning them in tea the colour of coal.
3 Thou shalt not . . . the congregation's enthusiasm by starting the service with phrases such as 'We are sinners!' or 'Repent or burn for eternity!'

King (of Kings)

Now that's quite a high status to hold if you ask me, and I feel that anyone capable of upholding that title is definitely worth following!

Kiss

A wonderfully enjoyable way of expressing your affection towards someone else! That is until you actually realise it is a really easy way of catching a cold or anything else for that matter! Its uses vary quite considerably. A peck on the cheek is often used as a way of saying 'I'm pleased to see you'. Grannies, however, appear to have developed a whole new technique which involves an introduction to the slobber monster from 32 Rose Petal Lane! This seemingly harmless old lady suddenly turns into a huge walking mouth producing two gallons of saliva every second and, with those immortal words which send shivers down any teenager's back – 'How about a kiss for Granny then?' – grabs you with the strength of a bodybuilder and plants a world-record-breaking, sloppy, squidgy smackeroo on your once clean, dry and totally innocent cheek! Lush! (Not!)

Various members of the youth group can also often be found in the dark areas of the church car-park exploring each other's tonsils with intense enthusiasm! Of course, the most famous kiss of all was dealt out by the winner of 'The Most Unpopular Person Ever' award, Judas. This sleaze betrayed Jesus with a kiss on the cheek. All for thirty pieces of silver. But, if Jesus was able to forgive those who crucified him, surely Judas was forgiven too?

Kitchen

Every church seems to have the same type of kitchen. You know, the one that is usually a shade of pale blue or yellow, has a cooker that doesn't work, three hundred kettles, forty thousand cups that are impossible to hold without burning your knuckles, a fridge that is never used, and a mysterious gang of ladies who appear at every coffee morning armed to the teeth with tea and biscuits!

Kross

Another example of how to be 'happening'. Simply replace the letter C with the letter K and you are at once a person who is hip. Various companies have adopted this approach believing it to be a new idea. How wrong they are! Remember those who wrote the Book of Psalms? Or those who write Hymns? Who said the church was out of touch?

Lamb

Incredibly delicious Sunday dinner! No, sorry, what I meant to say was that this is another of the many terms used for Jesus: the Lamb of God. Why? Well, Jesus was God's own sacrifice for us. To save us and give us a chance to get back on line and follow him. Quite an incredible thing to do really.

Lamentations

I guess I should know what this means and have something really witty to say about it. Unfortunately, I haven't the faintest idea and if you have then please write and tell me and I might include it in the second edition of this book . . . because we all know that it's going to be a huge blockbusting success, don't we?

Lamp

From the all-time favourite song of our Sunday School days: 'Give me oil in my lamp'. One of the many unusual songs sung at this time in your life, the all-time classic being 'Do your ears hang low, do they wobble to and fro'! What does it mean and why sing it at Sunday school? Who cares whether you can 'flip them over your shoulder like a regimental soldier' or not? Please, all you Sunday school teachers out there, stop using this song. If you can't do that, could you please explain it to me? Ta!

Last

As in 'The first shall be . . . and the . . . shall be first'. A cunning ploy is to use this at a Faith Supper where it is usually members of the youth group who get to the front of the queue first. You can usually find one or two 'really funny' old people who push in at the front using this classic phrase. What they fail to realise is that the youth group get to the front first knowing full well that they are bound to be suddenly overwhelmed by a barrage of old people singing this verse in unison. The youth group gets pushed to the back and, when they do eventually get to the table, will find very little left. Thus they have an excuse to visit the local chippy! Cunning, eh?

Late

As in '. . . for church'. Again, there are a few ways of coping with this:

1 The 'I hope no one notices' approach. Sneak in from the back of the church during a song where everyone else is jumping around and waving their hands up in the air!
2 The 'I'm sorry I'm late' approach. Can be done from the back or the front of the church as long as you enter trying to make yourself look as small as a very small thing indeed and occasionally catch the eye of someone in the congregation and give them that all-important 'I'm sorry' look.
3 The 'Look at me, everyone, I'm late' approach. Two variations: (a) `Burst in from the front of the church armed with five children you grabbed from outside and a pan of potatoes that you forgot to put on the cooker and say very loudly in a voice that says 'I've run all the way here' but with the words 'Sorry I'm late, everyone!' or (b) Saunter in from the back of the church wearing a huge smug grin, catching the eye of anything that moves with a look which says 'Yes, I know I'm late but I don't really care because I really am incredibly cool, aren't I?' Also try and catch the preacher's eye once you've sat down with the look that says 'Yes, I'm here now. You can get on with the service!'

Laugh

Some people seem to think that church is a place for eternal seriousness and solemnity, and that laughter in the church is wrong. Now, you try and tell me that a God who created this world full of all its wonderfully strange and weird creatures and plants hasn't got a sense of humour? Just look at yourself! Well, I disagree with the Anti-Humour League. God is probably the greatest practical joker of all who realised when he'd given out the five senses that something was missing . . . the sense of humour. If you ask me, it's the best of the lot!

Lazy

How we all feel on Easter morning and on Christmas Eve when we know we've got to go to those ridiculously early/late services! The great thing is once we get there it's a darn sight better than staying in at home! Lazy is also the feeling that takes over at rallies such as Spring Harvest where a week of praising God seems to mean going to forty lectures a day, ranging in topics from how prayer can help with the washing-up to how coffee mornings can be used to their full potential! There are also those services in the evening which last for approximately three years but if you go to the one for the young people it involves jumping around a lot to the sound of synthesisers, drums and guitars and shouting 'We love Jesus!' all the time! (Try it – it's fantastic fun!)

Life

Our time on this small lump of rotating rock in the middle of space. Many people seem to look at it as a huge drag. A monotonous existence with no meaning or purpose. Well, has Mrs. Miggins got news for you! Life is about adventure! Experiencing the ups and downs, the highs and the lows of the decisions we make and the paths we tread. Life is a huge unexplored wilderness unique to every individual. So don't hang around being a boring old stick-in-the-mud: look at every day as a way of experiencing something new and different . . . even if it is Mrs. Miggins' slide show on her days spent in Outer Mongolia, blah, blah, blah!

Light

Jesus is the Light of the World . . . and, boy, does it need one! This is a very good description really because no matter how dark it is even the light of the smallest candle can dispel that darkness. Isn't God clever? Light is also something that seems to suddenly get very lost and confused in those large cathedrals. Where does it go? The place is covered in windows, there is a profusion of candles all over the place and there are even thousands of brand-new light bulbs – but still no light! Even a torch advertised as having 1,000,000,000 candle power soon loses all interest in the situation, and the only light it seems to emit either disappears very quickly behind a large stone pillar or just sits in the torch and dribbles out of the end! It's no wonder that bishops wear those capes covered in millions of colours. If you fail to see an object that looks very similar to that spaceship from ET then you're bound to accidentally bump into him!

Looking

As in '. . . for a passage in the Bible'. Most embarrassing when standing at the front of the church to read the lesson for the day when you've forgotten what passage it was that you were looking for! There are a couple of ways of coping with this situation:

1 The 'No, I haven't forgotten which passage it was that I was looking for, honest, no really' approach. This involves standing at the front and searching at random until you come across the passage by mistake or the preacher reads out the name of it again 'for the benefit of the congregation'.
2 The 'Look at me, everybody, I've forgotten the passage that I'm supposed to be reading to you' approach. All this requires is the ability to grin at everyone and shout up to the preacher in a voice that says 'I know I'm an idiot but God still loves me' except with the words 'Guess what, everyone? I've forgotten the passage! Never mind, eh? You just talk amongst yourselves while I ask our wonderful preacher what it was, OK?' Unfortunately, even though it can prove to be effective on some occasions, it does have the disadvantage of getting the culprit banned from ever doing this all-important and enviable task again. (How diabolically upsetting for them!)

Lord's Prayer

It says it all. Praise, thanksgiving, asking for forgiveness. You name it and it's there. Jesus taught his disciples this one so I guess that it is pretty sorted as far as prayers go.

Lost

We always feel that we are but God knows different because he's found us!

Love

See that? That's God, that is!

Luke

Wrote one of the synoptic (now there's a fancy author-type word for you!) gospels. Also the name of the main character in the film *Star Wars*.

Lunch

As in 'Sunday . . .'. An excuse to leave church early and rush home 'because I've left the potatoes on!'

Lurve

Really cool way of saying love but has a slightly different meaning. You'd be very surprised if your great-granny came up to you and said something along the lines of 'I lurve you!' An overwhelming feeling to run away extremely quickly would undoubtedly take hold! But if that certain person that you've fancied for a while was to turn around one day and whisper in your ear, 'I lurve you!' you would suddenly feel very hot and start talking utter rubbish until your brain had grasped exactly what had happened!

Mad Preacher

A rare breed. Usually seen only once or twice a year, especially at Easter. There are two types, each easily recognised by their distinctive features:

Type One is the Hell Fire and Brimstone Preacher who is convinced that long, unkempt grey hair, white knuckles (caused by holding the edge of the pulpit very hard), and shouting a lot is very cool. He is usually armed with a huge leather Bible to wave above his head and to point at people with, while shouting 'We are sinners!', 'Aaallleeeelluuuiiaaaa!' or 'Aaaayyyyyymmeeyyyyeennnn!'

Type Two is the 'funny little run around the front of the church and make the children laugh' preacher. This one knows that even though he is small, slightly bald and wearing a less than trendy suit, his rosy cheeks, constant smile and contagious laugh will endear him to any congregation. Also has the ability to keep you awake, play the guitar, tell a joke and talk to the children – all at the same time.

Magazine
Any church worth its own steeple has one. Usually has an exotic title such as 'News from the Pews' or 'A Word about the Word'. Can contain gems such as the results of the flower-arranging contest, an in-depth report on how prayer can help your vegetable patch, and how much the raffle raised.

Malachi
These old words really do keep popping up, don't they?

Mark
See *Matthew*.

Matthew
See *Mark*.

Meditation
The popularity of this has increased due to the influence of a style of music and chanting known as 'Taizé'. Unfortunately, a few churches, not yet used to new ideas, have seen it as a type of affliction. For example, a young vicar keen to impress the locals of his new parish passed the word around that he was going to be having a meditation service every month in his study. At the first meeting, when everyone was sitting down, one of the ladies looked him in the eye and said, 'What's the matter with you, then?' The young vicar, a tad confused, asked her to explain. 'This 'ere medication meeting what we're having each month,' she said, 'I assumed there was something the matter with you so I brought this.' From her large tartan bag she removed a bottle of 'Oswald's Renowned Medication'. From that day on the vicar finds himself avoided by the locals muttering, 'Poor lad's got meditation.'

Micah
Sounds very similar to a crystal which, for those of you who have never done geology has a, er, umm, well, it has something very interesting and geological indeed about it but, as I don't want to confuse those of you who are uneducated and ignorant about the importance of geology, then I won't go into it. (Phew!) Anyway, back to Micah . . . so, who was he then? Anyone know? Anyone? Please? Look, you're going to make me look like a real thicky if you don't help me out? What do you mean: 'I know?!' Can I hear sniggering? Such a caring audience . . .

Microphone

This simple piece of technology has caused the creation of a rather annoying ritual. The user walks up to it, eyeing it from afar with caution. Once in receptive distance the user nods back and forth, puckering their lips and muttering far too quietly phrases such as 'Is it on?', 'I've never used one before' and 'Erm, errr, hello, er, ummmm, I, er, well, is it, oh, er, good!' Finally, before the speech can start, and having established that the volume is OK, the user must partake in a wrestling match with the stand (which always wins) and ends up straining their neck towards a microphone which is in completely the wrong position! And why is it that once all this has been done, the person behind the microphone shouts every single word?

Mighty

A brand of bread that seems to turn the consumer into the Incredible Hulk momentarily. (Should also be pronounced as, 'Moidy Woit!' while wearing a kangaroo.) Mmmmm . . . Would provide a most amusing effect if this was the case and slices of 'Moidy Woit' were accidentally used for communion bread. The unsuspecting priest passes out the innocent-looking cube of goodness to sweet old Mrs. Goddard who, having received the bread and wine, leaves to go back to her seat. Unfortunately, she forgets to let go of the communion rail and finds herself back in her seat with half a tree, whilst elsewhere the bread has taken effect on the youth group . . . and I'll let your imagination decide what happens next!

Miracles

Common in the New Testament and also found in many parts of the Old Testament. Jesus excelled at them. The disciples tried to do them – and often succeeded with his help. Advanced miracles included feeding five thousand people with 'what mum gave me for dinner' and walking on water. Peter nearly managed the second of these – that was until he realised that unless you're the Son of God it's actually not that easy to do.

Missing

Many things go missing from church. The rhythm is often missing from the singing. Interest can go missing during the sermon. The youth group are often missing something, even though they're there, and the congregation sometimes misses the point of being there at all. Thankfully, God is never missing from anything.

Moses

Extremely hard bloke from the Old Testament. The kind of bloke you'd want on your side in a fight. The kind of bloke who doesn't mess around with threats such as 'If you don't move, I might have to break something on your head' but instead uses ones such as 'If you don't do what God tells you then I might just have to arrange for a plague of locusts to get a bit clumsy like.'

Music

The real cause of the one true 'Holy War'. The battle has raged for many a year, new powers appearing along the way. The lovers of organ music hold their ground, the trenches dug well in, as behind them come the reinforcements of the choir. Opposing them stand the followers of Kendrick, armed to the dog-collar with twelve-string guitars and tracts. And in no-man's-land sit the congregation, attacked from both sides and unable to decide which side they prefer as both have some good ideas.

Nahum
Exactly. Just what I would have said. Couldn't agree more. Brilliant.

Nehemiah
Apparently he's in the Bible too. Maybe this could be a new game: 'Spot the Nehemiah'?

Neighbour
As in 'Thou shalt love thy . . .'. Another one of Jesus' sermon points which sound so simple until put into practice. He obviously never met my neighbour.

New
As in '. . . Vicar/Minister/Priest'. Easily recognised by the 'I'm on a diet' badge worn two weeks into their appointment having been invited for tea to everybody's house in the circuit/parish.

Night
It is well known that Jesus will come again like a 'thief in the night'. This does not mean that you will wake up to find all your silver spoons missing and an apparent lack of electrical entertainment appliances in the front room. Oh no. Those who do wake up will find that there is a definite lack of people in the world and will wish they had been taken too. Still, the warning has been sent so no one can turn around and say that they didn't know it was going to happen. For that we should all be grateful. There aren't many thieves who tell you exactly what they're going to do!

No Room

Said by the winner of the 'Most Unpopular Barman' award. One can hardly see his business growing after such an event. 'So you're the one who turned away the King of Kings' must be a phrase that haunted him for the rest of his life.

Nose

Innocent cause of an infliction commonly known as 'Pewitis' or 'Primary Rebounding Above the Young person's Elementary Resonance Source' (PRAYERS for short). The visual sign of this is either a slight reddening of the forehead or a bruise which draws a line from one side of the forehead to the other. It often strikes after the words 'Let us pray', upon which a member of the congregation, while lowering to a comfortable praying position, is instantly and without warning attacked by the 'Sneeze from Beelzebub's Abode'. This throws the body into a sharp up-and-down movement and brings the forehead into direct contact with the pew in front. The result is the above-mentioned characteristic mark on the forehead.

Notice Board

Should be renamed as the 'Obvious Board' or the 'Look at me, everyone, here I am!' board. Often dominates the rear of the church and is usually a foot deep in out-of-date information. People appear to have an aversion to taking down notices and instead hide them with yet another notice. Why? Are they afraid that the individual who placed the notice entitled 'Coffee evening with CAKE!' is going to be tragically removed from reality upon the discovery that it has been taken down three months after the event? I think not.

Obadiah

The Bible is full of names used by no one any more. This is one of them. Just imagine how cool it would be though to be called Obadiah. So much better than Martin or Trevor. The amount of street cred you'd get! Obviously, the Bible times were full of incredibly cool people who not only followed God but also had great names!

Offer

Jesus invites everyone to offer themselves to him. Basically he wants us to give him all that we are now, all that we have been and all that we will become. He wants the good and the bad, the bits we want to forget, even our secrets. Everything that we are, he is asking us to give to him! Isn't that amazing?

Old

It is a well-known fact that churches attract old people. They sit in the back four rows of every church wearing three-piece suits and hats that look like sleeping cats. What is even stranger is that, wherever you go, these people are replicated. They are everywhere. Maybe it is some secret underground movement. Armed with their bags of boiled sweets, personalised cushions and a passionate yearning to warble loudly to all the old hymns, they aim to infiltrate every denomination and make us all follow the way of Pew Ownership.

Organ

The Exocet missile of the Church. Due to technological advances this weapon has decreased in size considerably. No longer are we overwhelmed by the vast mechanical wonders that filled half the church and sucked in the congregation when warming up. Now we find ourselves faced with a wafer-thin biscuit of an affair. Black and sleek in design, flashing lights and lots of buttons. Words such as 'midi' and 'percussion' mix happily with effects like 'repeat' and 'whizzer'. No annoying pedals to keep the thing going. No need for a separate generator, yet enough power to wake any congregation at a distance of five miles.

Organist

Old, grey haired and completely insane. These people have bonded with their instrument to such a degree that they have actually become a part of the machine. Innocent they may appear, but once they sit down on that stool they are sucked into a completely different dimension: an existence where they spend their days running up and down vast flights of keyboards shouting 'I prefer the old tune!' and 'Who's moved my mirror?' I don't know if anyone else has noticed but as soon as they sit down they grow another set of legs and then do an impression of a herd of gazelles running across a cattle grid!

Outside Services

Something you find yourself at but are never really too sure how you got there. The Order of Service is duplicated on to a sheet of pink or blue paper which gets damp as it starts to rain. The songs are led by the choirmaster on his penny whistle, which is all very well until he suddenly thinks he is in an Irish folk band and starts to jazz it up. Everyone has dressed for the occasion and then covered themselves with masses of coats, scarves and hats. The visiting preacher can't be heard and the flower arrangement has just settled rather neatly in Mrs. Bartholomew's hair. However, such an event is usually a great excuse for a nosh-up inside the chapel afterwards at which everyone overheats because the heating was left on all day! In't God's people brilliant?

Parking

Although obviously a new and innovative idea, parking is yet to be provided at many churches. All you get is two and a half acres of wonderfully cared-for gardens and a footpath that escapee children run up and down during all the quiet services. If you do manage to persuade the WI (they seem to be in charge of everything) that a car park is necessary, be prepared for it to be at the back of the church and only accessible to those who drive cars smaller than a pram. Of course, the only way to provide space for a car park is to tarmac the vicar's garden.

Past

Many people seem to think that the church is stuck in the past, that it refuses to move with the times and is only interested in sitting in its comfortable chair of tradition, reading the well-thumbed book of ignorance. This is not true. The Church is anything but stuck in the past. It is in fact running like blazes to try and keep up with the billions of members of the Family of God. There's Sunday school, youth groups, drama groups, mission groups, choir evenings, worship teams, welcomers, mission plans, fund-raisers, prayer meetings, and that's just on Monday evening! The Church is alive, so next time you have the urge to check its heartbeat, be warned: it may smack you across the room!

Pastor

One of the many names used for the person who runs the show. Can be male or female unless you are of the view that men and women are not equal and unaware that you are totally wrong. They wear anything from the huge, colourful, all-flashing, all-covering tent to the 'cool for cats' cartoon waistcoat and glow-in-the-dark dog-collar, and are more often than not overworked, expected to do everything, and still be full of love for everyone.

Peace

This is brilliant! Peace is a great idea, be it worldwide or just something you hope someone has and therefore tell them so. However, the 'giving of the peace' is something entirely different. It is more a giving of the 'awkward feeling' or the presenting of the 'please don't catch my eye'. Catholics have this sussed. With open arms and big smiles they shake each other's hands every week and give the peace. It's wonderful, friendly and very good for everyone. However, other churches can find it all a bit odd, especially if they are not used to 'giving it'. If you ever get the chance, just sit in on one of these services and watch. Everyone has spotted the fateful words in the Order of Service: 'The peace shall be given'. As the time gets closer and closer, the nervous shuffling has been replaced with nervous 'not moving at all, thank you very much'. The silence gets heavier and heavier. Even the tornado-sized bluebottle fly has come to rest and quickly squeezed into the piles of paper pinned to the poster board. Finally the minister announces the dreaded act and stands back to soak up the heady love-filled atmosphere created by people all standing as straight as a board, refusing to move from their pew and only shaking the hands of those within fingers' reach. We really are a funny bunch aren't we?

Pew

As already discussed, these should be replaced by chairs which are comfy, because pews aren't. However, pews have many other interesting points to consider. For a start, many are covered in graffiti of some type, though I have yet to be at a service where I have either seen this act take place or heard a member of 'Thy Neighbour's Pew Watch' stand up and grab the culprit. Odd. Also, a piece of the church's original carpet often finds new life as a cushion. Such luxury. And why is it that people still spend the first half of the service trying to get the notice sheet to stand in the book rest knowing full well that it always slips out of the bottom? Oh, and there's no leg room . . .

Pope

Head of the Roman Catholic Church. Not much more you can say really because that is such an awe-inspiring position to be in. To be chosen to be Head of the Church anywhere is enough. For example, just look at the importance placed on leaders in your local God Spot. We all know about Mrs. Miggins but what about people like the Sunday school leaders. The real proof of the importance of a particular job is to see how quickly people volunteer to take over if someone has to leave. Now the more important a job is, the less keen people are to step in because they know that they will actually have to do something. Stand up in church and announce that a new Sunday school leader is needed and witness the amazing transformation that takes place. No one will look at you because suddenly, for the first time since the church was built, an interesting article has appeared on the notice sheet. Exactly. If being a Sunday school leader is so hard, imagine being the Pope. Respect due.

Praise

How many ways are there to do this? Well, there are more than 'on the trumpet and harp'. Praising God can be done anywhere, any time. Just a quick mutter at work, or in the middle of an essay, to say to God how great you think he is. How about a serious knees-up at church or perhaps a quiet prayer-time? Not enough? Well, go for a walk in the countryside and thank God for the world, or the next time you are out with friends just say a quick silent prayer thanking God for each of them. Praise comes in all shapes and forms. Your whole life is one huge living praise so why not try and make it the loudest, tambourine and twelve-string-guitared praise that you can!

Prayer

Now, this really is worth talking about! God in his insurmountable wisdom decided that chatting with his creation was a good idea. He wished to converse, to talk, to share with us, his creation. Moreover, he wanted us to have a deep and personal relationship with him. 'It's good to talk' is not just true of telephones. Talking to God is free. You can do it wherever you are. You can talk about anything you like (God is God after all, and you are hardly in a position to shock the Creator), and the more you talk the better the relationship gets. So have a go. It's freer than an 0800 number and more important than fresh underwear, and God never ever hangs up. We may think he does but what actually happens is that we leave the room and forget that the phone is off the hook only to return to find God waiting patiently. I just love him, don't you?

Psalms

See *Hymns*.

Pulpit

I have always thought it odd that a church which loves making sure its ministers are as obvious as a toenail in an ice cream, dressing them up to look like a walking fairground attraction, then proceeds to make them stand out even more by putting them in a box ten feet above the congregation. From the back of the church all this achieves is to make the poor soul look like one of those amusing erasers you find donning the tops of most pencils in primary schools.

Quiet

Everybody thinks everybody else should be. Children should be quiet when in church. The youth group should sit quietly, no matter how funny it is to time how long it takes for Mr. and Mrs. Adams to do their narrated bible readings. The choir should always sing the third verse of number 526 quietly. Church in general should be quiet with a capital Q 'or I'll tell your mum and dad because I know where they live'. So why is the organ so big? Why is laughing so much fun? Why is singing God's praises and dancing while whacking a tambourine on your head such an ace feeling? Quiet has its place but so does yelling out for God. After all, his love is hard to keep quiet about!

Quit

Something God never does, even though we do our best to show him some quite superb examples of how to do it. We quit following him, listening to him, helping others, taking his advice, praying, learning, discovering and progressing, and that's just before breakfast. Ask God if he has ever quit anything and he'll probably tell you that the only thing he has ever quit is taking Moses out to lunch because all Moses ever says after a few glasses of mead is '. . . and when the seas parted, right, I just turned to look at the ever-closing chariots and laughed my pants off' – and even then God would be joking. I tell God the same things again and again and again and I'm convinced he's as interested this time as the last. So there you go: God doesn't quit, he just carries on loving you forever. Brilliant!

Quite

Word used to help describe any activity that wasn't all that successful. For example, the prayer meetings on Thursday mornings have been 'quite' successful because, even though they were only attended by the vicar, they show that the Lord is truly beginning to move.

Rave

Becoming increasingly popular among younger Christians. The idea is to worship God in a way that they can express themselves. For some reason, getting a sore bum in a cold church during a distant sermon and singing slow hymns doesn't quite do it for the generation of 'bombastic jazz bass lines' and 'sorted saands camin' at ya fru da slammin' tracks, man'. Anyway, the basic idea is to cover the church hall with large tye-dyed sheets, hire a smoke machine and some lights, and then praise like crazy, dance for Jesus and revel in the love of God! What a great idea! Of course, there is still a need for quiet services but have a 'rave' once a month, get a few of the 'oldies' to go and who knows what may happen. After all, the Church is a family!

Reach

Reaching out for something generally requires effort. This could be reaching out to get the jam off the top shelf for mum which results in physical effort. However, reaching out for someone requires a lot more. It takes risk of self. But just remember what it is like when you are in need and someone reaches out for you. A close friend puts their arms around you or just listens. When you need to cry and there is no sense of awkwardness, just love and support. That is reaching out. Not expecting a reward, just giving someone your love. Isn't that a great idea? You see, God reached out to us through Jesus, and Jesus reaches out to us everywhere we go. Not just in a supportive role, but giving us the opportunity to reach out to others. To show them a little of what it is all about. That is reaching out. That is love, and that is what our faith is all about. Letting the love of God shine through us in the world as we reach out for those around us, wherever we are and whenever we are. Yet another one of God's simple but absolutely amazing ideas!

Readers

Why is it that anyone who reads the Bible out at church goes up to the front all meek and mild but then, once in front of the lectern, develops the kind of voice used only in trailers for video releases? Meek Mrs. Fanshaw, who usually speaks so quietly it would be easier to hear her if you were sitting in her mouth, suddenly booms down the microphone with a voice that makes you duck for cover, half expecting the back of the church to blow up and Arnie to run in armed to the teeth! Still, it certainly makes it all a lot more interesting, especially if the reader happens to be reading one of the really gory bits from the Old Testament.

Reading

Asking someone to do this has the same effect as standing up at church and telling a very rude (but probably rather funny) joke. People look at you in horror. You have suddenly transformed from a 'lovely Christian kid' to someone who 'oh, ohhh, oOOOHHHH Howcouldhel'veneverheardanythinglikeit inallmylife!' I don't understand it. We are taught to read aloud at school. We spend hours speaking in public in our everyday lives but just ask someone to read 'Mark 1 verses 2 to 4' and you are in for trouble and usually end up doing it yourself. Weird.

Recital

I hate these. I know I shouldn't hate anything and I've tried. But sitting at church and being forced to listen to Mr. Wiggins, the only trained singer in the choir (there is always one and usually no more), do his recital of 'that ol' rugged cross (a spiritual)' drives me barmy. I do not need to hear it. I do not want to hear it. But I have to hear it. I tell you, if he sings 'Swing low, sweet chaaaaaaarrrriiiiiiiiiooooooot' it'll end up swinging lower than he could ever imagine, I can tell you.

Rest

Sunday is a day of rest because God said so. So next time you are lazing in front of the fire on a Sunday afternoon watching one of those great Doris Day (I want to marry her) movies and your parents or wife or partner or 'significant other' tells you to stop being lazy and do something, ignore them. Just point out that God said you could so you are going to do what he says.

Revelation

The scary bit at the end of the Bible but also the good bit . . . God wins! Contains some great characters too such as the Four Riders of the Apocalypse. Now these really are scary guys. Big horses and enough power to destroy the world. Ouch. Even harder than a dinner lady. Probably.

Sad

I don't like feeling sad. Nobody likes feeling sad. So many things can make you feel sad. From a film on TV to breaking up with someone. Crying helps but God can help more. Sometimes it seems like he just isn't there. When times are just so bad that there are no right answers. When there is no help anyone can give you. When there seems to be no way out. When every waking moment is filled with a bad memory, or a good one that makes you even more sad. But he is there. It takes time and life can be not what you want at times, but talk to God about it. God is in every little thing that helps you along, from the phone call from a close friend to the smell of fresh air when you wake up in the morning. God doesn't like you feeling sad either, so tell him about it when you are. He understands.

Safe

That's what you are when you know God loves you!

Saint

Cool bloke, great suits, nice car. Also, someone who does amazing things for God. Mother Theresa. Martin Luther King. They speak for themselves.

Salvation

A big word that basically means that you have accepted God into your life for ever. You don't need to be struck down. You don't need to go forward at a big rally. These can help some people but don't think that you've done it wrong if you say 'yes' to Jesus and there are no flashing lights. Remember how he called his disciples? Just walking along a beach and there they were. One introduction and they joined him. No lights or falling down, just a big 'YES' to Jesus. If you do that then you are in for one terrific life!

Samson

A big man. A big, BIG man. A big, BIG, hard, 'wouldn't want me to get a bit clumsy' man. So hard he killed a lion on his own. So hard that no one, seeing that he had huge amounts of long hair, said, 'Tha' looks like a right grit jess wi' 'air all long an' flowin', lad.' That is until Delilah found out that his strength lay in the self-same long hair. She cut it off and then everyone laughed at weak old Samson, shouting, 'Oi, Sammy boy, tha' looks like a right grit jess wi' 'air all short an' spiky lad.' Samson had the last laugh though. Obviously he had been caught by very stupid people. So stupid in fact that although they realised Samson needed long hair to be strong, when they brought him out at the party for a good old giggle at 'old short hair, no strength', they didn't look and think, 'Hmm, he now has the long hair of much strength and I must run away.' Oh, no. Instead, they looked at him and thought, 'Hmm, he . . . oh dear, . . . splat!' as Samson pushed the pillars over and brought the whole place crashing to the ground, killing everyone including himself. A very hard man indeed.

Seat

Passed down from generation to generation, the family seat at church is a most valued possession. Not likely to appear on the Antiques Roadshow but you try telling that to Mrs. Greystone who, given the chance, would probably build over it an ornate four-poster canopy with velour blinds, heated cushions, teasmade and hymn book dispenser (not forgetting the secret compartment for the ever-so-important supply of contraband butterscotch sweets).

Sex

One of the most beautiful things our Creator ever gave us. The most wonderful way to express and share love in marriage and continue the human race. Unfortunately, in many areas of life it has become something you can buy off the top shelf. The emotion, the love, the sharing are removed and all that remains is the physical thrill. I am not decrying the physical thrill; it's just that without the other ingredients sex is nothing more than a carnival ride. Sex is a beautiful gift. Let's do our best to keep it that way. God knows we are not perfect. He knows the pressures. All we need to do is to accept that he is right and deal with it together.

Shake

As in '. . . hands'. This happens at every church door. Up the steps you go, innocent of the anguish you will soon experience. The door is open and in front of you stand vast numbers of people with Colgate smiles, hymn books and notice sheets. You approach tentatively. They approach vigorously. You take your hand from your pocket. They jump for it. One makes contact. You've had it. Your left hand is suddenly full of books and pieces of paper so you are totally defenceless as your right hand has each joint shaken into oblivion. Welcome to church and don't say that I didn't warn you.

Sin

Uh oh. Don't go near there. That's naughtiness and badness and 'waking mum and dad at half past two in the morning'-ness. Still, we all do it. From stealing an extra biscuit at Aunt Edie's to lustful thoughts. God doesn't like it. Don't do it. Hear endeth the lesson.

Singing

Singing at church is, to say the least, interesting. No matter what the tune, if you listen carefully you will notice a multitude of different approaches to turning Hymn 235 into something resembling the music off the Old Spice advert being sung in fourteen different languages, at different speeds and varying time signatures. The Sunday School are all singing in their 'Good morning, Mrs. Underwood' voices. The choir are convinced that even though there are only seven members, they sound 'just like that gospel choir on *Songs of Praise* last week'. The Youth Group have decided that singing is 'uncool', and anyway, all the lads' voices are breaking. Then there is the rest of the congregation with its own selection of warblers, wailers and completely out-of-tuners! Nice . . .

Sit

Necessary in church but also impossible when you experiences the 'pew seat blues':

> Cos I've got the pew seat blues (oh yeah)
> and I can't sit down on their hardness no more.

I've got the pew seat blues (dah dah dah da)
and I can't take no carpet cushions no more.
Yeah I've got the pew seat blues (impressive piano bit)
and I'm gonna pray they buy real seats soon (piano)
wooo yeah.

Slow

The last five minutes of the service, any hymn with more than three choruses, the Sunday school coming into church, the choir singing 'Shine, Jesus, shine', the second reading of the day . . .

Son of God

See that? That's Jesus, that is! Imagine being the Son of God! I can't and you can't, so perhaps we shouldn't. However, that's who he is and someone who can raise the dead, take on a temple full of traders alone, rise again on the third day after being put to death, and proclaim that the greatest thing is 'love' is definitely worth following.

Song of Solomon

Poetic, strange and at times downright outrageous! Solomon must have really been in love, as in 'ell, youu, arrr, veee, eeee: LURVE!'

Special Services

These are the nearest the church ever gets to cabaret. Anyone who can do anything in the church usually ends up doing it at one of these. They are great fun! I love it when all parts of the church get together to share a bit of what they all are. The youth group do a sketch that goes wrong and everyone laughs. The choir sings a few songs and everyone joins in. The young ones in Sunday school say a few poems and everyone applauds. The minister doesn't do a sermon and everyone is relieved. A great way for the church to let everyone see that it is a family.

Stable

Jesus was born in one. Not nice. Not very National Health but there you go. God is God and can be as unconventional as he wants, I guess. But that's it, isn't it? The whole point was that Jesus was God made human. If he had been born a king we would never have been able to relate to him. We would have followed not because we wanted to but because we thought we had to. Yet again, a brilliant idea.

Steward

These are usually respectable people in the church who stand at the door and welcome people, or do other jobs like taking the collection. However, at my old church we changed all this and put Pete up there. He is giant of a man with long hair, the scariest facial hair I have ever seen, and an intriguing denim jacket. Now that's a welcome! If God loves Pete we all know that we are safe!

Tea

I am a Methodist. I have been brought up in a church which exists only because there is tea. If there wasn't then we would have no way to start our meetings or end our services. We would have no lifeline. Tea is a way of life. We have kitchens and thousands of staff members dedicated to making tea. We have special teapots which hold enough tea for a thousand people yet can be miraculously carried by one person aged eighty-three. We believe that it enhances our minds, enabling us to decide upon important issues such as the rota for making sure that the minister's glass of water is always fresh. We believe that if you don't drink tea then there is something wrong with you. Tea is . . . therefore I am a Methodist.

Time with God

Now this really is important. The weird thing is that time with God is always happening and never ceases. He is everywhere all the time so there is no such thing as time without God. But time with God also means talking and sharing with God, and experiencing who and what he is. You can do this whenever you want but it is best to make sure that you give him some quality time. Unfortunately, I seem to have convinced myself that quality time is just before I go to sleep. Yeah, right, like I'm really able to communicate. Not brilliant and I try to make other time too, but falling asleep with God is actually rather cool!

Titus

Wot a silly name.

Toilets

The ladies' toilets are always clean, warm, freshly painted and inside the church. The gents' toilets are always dusty, freezing cold, freshly decorated during the last ice age and outside. Again, one of those things with no explanation, it just is. In the same vein as keeping all the brass hinges for the umbrella stands at the end of pews even though the actual stands were removed during the war for weapons construction.

Toy Box

You have children? You want to bring them to church? Well, worry ye not for behold, here is a product of much use! A box which is impossible to carry, full of toys that won't go back in once they are taken out! Take up a pew for yourselves and an aisle as well! Why not take up the front of the church and drown out the sermon? The all new Toy Box! Get one and get noticed!

Uncomfortable

Pews are uncomfortable. So replace them. Replace them with chairs which have cushions, chairs that recline, chairs that do not require a sitting position of ninety degrees. Many churches have replaced their pews. Indeed, modern churches are being built with chairs that you can move about. This is great, I hear you cry, a move in the right direction. Well, this move in the right direction has brought about the discovery of the only advantage of pews. Elbow room was never a problem. More often than not you could sit and sprawl a bit, do a little stretch. Not any more. The almighty chairs of convenience and comfort which cunningly interlock with each other have a drawback. No elbow room. There is no allowance for the need to remove sweets from a pocket. There is no space to scratch that awkward rib. There isn't even enough room to stand up and hold your hymn book sensibly. Maybe what we need are comfortable, collapsible pews? Well, it doesn't really matter, does it? It's all a bit of a laugh!

Understand

Why do we always seem to be trying to understand what God is doing? He is God. We are not. How are we ever going to be able to grasp exactly what he is doing and why? We can't. However, we can try to understand a little. We can understand the need to love each other. We can understand that we should help each other. But there are some things I will never understand. Why did God allow wasps to evolve? Why doesn't someone tell flies that it is impossible to fly through glass? Why do old men get hairy ears?

Unusual

That feeling you get when you are sitting in church having not listened to a word the minister has said. The feeling that you suddenly become aware of while counting the shades of green in the stained glass window at the front. The feeling that makes you look around you and realise that God is real. It doesn't happen much but when it does everything suddenly makes sense even though you aren't quite sure what it actually is. You just know that God is real and he loves you! This feeling can happen anywhere. When you are in the bath or out walking or having a drink with a few friends. Well, that's God for you. Unexpected and not likely to turn up when we think he should.

Vestry

The room of sacred power. Only the church secretary, the minister and an old woman are allowed in. The door is often locked. The walls are usually adorned with scary pictures of Victorian people who look important but no one can remember why. The cupboards contain valuables like the hymn numbers, a few extra wires for something that is no longer in church, a Bible, a broken collection plate, and the dusty plans for the new hall. The furniture is sparse: a chair from the Middle Ages, a chair from the Sunday school room, a rug inscribed with a passage from the Bible, and a table more suited to a game of cards. Oh, and it is usually smaller than the pulpit.

Vicarage

Biggest house in the village. Huge in fact. Large gardens, stables, five bedrooms and only one room that can ever be kept warm. These places often contain a wonderful display of house decorating through the ages. You see, very few circuits or parishes, or whatever you call them, like to admit that the vicarage needs decorating or tidying up, or perhaps connecting to the local electrical grid. Phrases such as 'new carpets' or 'worn curtains' and, at the very worst, 'a shower unit' strike fear into the heart of any church treasurer. Who cares that the front room is floral whilst the kitchen is a nice purple? Does it really matter that when you walk up the stairs the carpet comes off? What is wrong with an outside toilet, a bath that takes off your skin, and a heating system which requires the world's supply of coal to keep going? Nothing, except that you feel as though you are living in three or four different time zones at once, that you have to wear wellies to go to the loo, and that the only way to stay warm is to never ever go out into the hall.

Vicar's Wife

Too many types to know where to start. The most obvious is the one that looks and acts more like the vicar than the vicar does. Very keen on wearing purple suits with dodgy hats and usually involved in every church meeting from the day she arrives with the words, 'I like the rose bushes to be perfect'.

Also, you will notice that she never actually speaks to you. You can stand there trying to make conversation with the female version of Genghis Khan but all you get is a face staring right through and into your soul. She wants to know if you have any nasty thoughts about the members of the Keep Our Church Brown Society or whether you were the one who put clingfilm over all the toilets. Then there is the other extreme. The 'isn't she lovely?' vicar's wife. She makes a point of not trying to take over her husband's job. She smiles a lot and is actively involved in church rather than trying to get the church actively involved in her. She does not do flower arranging all the time and is more than happy to allow the youth group to stay late drinking coffee. Of course, there are those in the middle who are a mixture of both. Unfortunately I haven't met any of them but I have met far too many of the 'I am in charge' vicar's wife and only a few of the 'Of course you can, dear' vicar's wife. Funny that.

Virgin Birth

Amazing. Incredibly hard to comprehend as it is impossible to do unless you are God. Of course, a few forget that God can do the impossible and make statements like 'I believe in God but I think the bit about the virgin birth is a tad far-fetched'. Why? Because it's a bit too unbelievable and the kind of thing only God can do? That's his job! God does 'God-type' things. Look, if Jesus can heal the sick, raise the dead and invent the cheapest home brew, then I am sure that his dad can do some equally impressive things too! Some people, eh?

Wally

Every church has one, almost as if it's a package deal: '... and remember, not only the keys to the church, but your very own wally too!' They're the ones who always appear to be doing something but no one actually knows what. They're at every meeting, prayer group, slide show and coffee morning but no one knows why because they never do anything. Also have a habit of turning up late, leaving during the middle of the sermon, dropping their hymn book and singing out of tune. Usually devoid of a name and often referred to as: 'excuse me,' 'oh, hello,' and 'erm, would you mind ...'

Warm

Approximately minus ten degrees if you are the church treasurer. This man often uses phrases like, 'Well, we didn't even have a heating system when I was a lad at this church.' Yeah, but what is the point of having a heating system if you don't turn the bloomin' thing on?

Weddings

Don't do it! Don't throw away your freedom! Run away! Apart from that, weddings are great. Loads of people get together to celebrate the fact that two people are so completely in love that they are willing to give their entire life to another person. Isn't that amazing? I can't imagine anyone loving me that much!

Welcome

You should know all about this by now. We've talked about every aspect of welcoming people into church, so if you've forgotten any of it you can just read it again. Of course, it is always worth remembering that we are always welcome to God's love. No matter how yucky we are, if we say sorry from the depths of all that we are, then we are forgiven and thus experience God's love. It's not really something you can be funny about because it is just so incredible.

Wine

Catholics drink gallons of the stuff which is strong enough to take rust off. Evangelicals do the same. And Methodists do something completely ridiculous. They pour minute amounts of Ribena into thimbles. I am a Methodist and, although I know about their dislike for the evils of alcohol, I do think that someone somewhere should stand up and tell whoever is in charge that thimbles of blackcurrant cordial are not the same as a taste of wine and not nearly as significant. Honestly, some people!

Wisdom

God has oodles of this! I guess that's what being God is about.

Women's Groups

Well, have I opened up a whole wasps' nest or what? How many men's groups are there at church? Very few indeed! But the women's groups have become an integral part of church life. It's not that all the groups are strictly for women, except of course the Women's Group, but then that's rather obvious. Other groups appear which men just don't go to, for example, flower arranging and coffee morning organising. I can understand the flower-arranging bit, but come on, lads, sort it out! Why not an evening of Motorcycle Appreciation, or Beers of the World and how to brew them? All you need is a bit of imagination.

Xmas

It is not 'Xmas'; it is Christmas. I do not know why it was shortened to an 'X' but it really does get on my wick. I guess it's all part of the increasing commercialisation of Christmas. It all starts ten months early and costs everyone far too much money. Presents do not need to be expensive. You should be able to open a present and see why it was given. The thought should be an essential

part of the giving and receiving. Of course, in my house you can always tell the presents from me because they are completely useless and very silly. You don't believe me? Well, how does a five-foot inflatable banana sound? I think it's a family trait. I once received a ginormous parcel which when unwrapped was nothing more than a chocolate bar. A weird family but at least for us Christmas is a time for fun rather than debt and outdoing the neighbours.

X

What more can I do with 'X'? Very little in the church begins with it. What a cool letter! It's an essential part of our alphabet but can't even be bothered to have more than a few of its own words. Even when it does it is so lazy that it hides behind the sound of another letter, for example xylophone and xenophobic. Cool or what?

Yawn
Church is the best place to start a bout of the yawns. If you can get the preacher to yawn, even better.

You
Oi, YOU! God loves ya!

Yule-type Cheer
Christmas is a time for happiness. We remember the birth of Jesus and celebrate by giving each other presents, eating, drinking and generally having a good time. How lovely. But what about those who are lonely? The homeless? Christmas is a time to remember the fact that Jesus was born in a shed at the back of a hotel which was too full to allow a pregnant girl inside into the warmth. Now if there was ever an allegory of the world we live in . . .

Zebedee

Springy bloke off 'The Magic Roundabout' with a weird moustache. Odd that the father of James and John was named after him.

Zebulen, Zedekiah, Zerah, Zerubbabel, Zeruiah, Ziba, Ziklag, Zimri, Zin, Zobah, Zorah

I never realised that the Bible had such great words in it. Check it out, especially if you want to understand what the preacher is saying, what God is saying, or if you need to find a decent and original name for your band.

Zechariah

Well, I have just found out that this was John the Baptist's father. Isn't it great what you learn if you actually sit down and read the Bible a little? You can come up with amazing facts to tell your mates!

Zee End

That's all, folks, see you next book. Just remember that believing in Jesus and following him isn't dull, uninteresting and extraordinarily un-amusing. It is mad, crazy, exciting, frightening and very funny. So next time you feel that everything is a bit shoddy, look in the mirror and spend a few minutes pulling stupid faces while yelling, 'Jesus loves me!' You'll soon see the funny side!

Slide show anyone?
...anyone...
HEBRIDES
BOX XVII